Engraved in Flesh

ויאמר אלהים אל-אברהם ואתה את-בריתי תשמר אתה וזרעך אחריך לדרתם: זאת בריתי אשר תשמרו ביני וביניכם ובין זרעך אחריך המול לכם כל-זכר: ונמלתם את בשר ערלתכם והיה לאות ברית ביני וביניכם: ובן שמונת ימים ימול לכם כל-זכר לדרתכם...

Genesis 17:9–12

ויהי בדרך במלון ויפגשהו ה׳ ויבקש המיתו: ותקח צפרה צר ותכרת את-ערלת בנה ותגע לרגליו ותאמר כי חתן-דמים אתה לי: וירף ממנו אז אמרה חתן דמים למולת:

Exodus 4:24–6

Engraved in Flesh

Piotr Rawicz and his novel *Blood from the Sky*

ANTHONY RUDOLF

MENARD PRESS
2007

First published in 1996 by Menard Press,
8 The Oaks, Woodside Avenue, London N12 8AR
This revised edition published in 2007

Cover: 'Expulsion' by R. B, Kitaj
© 2007 R. B. Kitaj, c/o Marlborough Gallery, London W1S 4BY
Frontispiece: 'Abraham' by R. B. Kitaj
© 1992 R. B. Kitaj, c/o Marlborough Gallery, London W1S 4BY
Photographs: Sergei Kravtsov and llya Levin (see acknowledgements)

For full copyright information see acknowledgements on page 94–6

Representation
Inpress Limited, Northumberland House
11 The Pavement, Popes Lane, Ealing, London W5 4NG
Tel: 020 8832 7464 Fax: 020 8832 7465
E-mail: stephanie@inpressbooks.co.uk
www.inpressbooks.co.uk

Worldwide Distribution (except North America)
Central Books (Troika), 99 Wallis Road
Hackney Wick, London E9 5LN
Tel: 020 8986 4854
www.centralbooks.com

Distribution in North America
Small Press Distribution Inc.
1341 Seventh Street, Berkeley, CA 94710, USA
www.spdbooks.org

ISBN 978 1 874320 57 9

Typeset by Antony Gray
Scanning by Tony Frazer
Printed in Great Britain by
Cambridge University Press Printing

Contents

Prefatory Note

Engraved in Flesh is in five linked sections. It deals mainly with one of the two published books by Piotr Rawicz, translated as *Blood from the Sky*. Section 1 is a general essay about the novel and its intellectual, historical, religious and literary matrices: it is keyed both with *numbers*, referring to footnotes at the end of the section, and with *letters*, referring to the accounts of the author's life and times that form Section 3 of the book.

Section 2 consists of a detailed description of the novel interspersed with a running commentary and some key quotes. Section 4 contains my translations of various short texts by Rawicz, including brief excerpts from his second and final published book, *Bloc-notes d'un contre-révolutionnaire*. Section 5 is a detailed and commented bibliography.

All texts mentioned throughout the book are listed, and sometimes described, in the bibliography.

Rather than read Section 1 straight through (plus the numbered notes) and only then 'read the life' detailed in Section 3, the reader is encouraged to interrupt the reading of Section 1 by turning to Section 3 at the appropriate lettered signals. But it is also possible to read the book in a linear fashion.

This short book is one of a continuing series of texts engaging with issues arising from World War Two. In the first of them, a study of Primo Levi (1990), I stated in a note that I hoped one day to write about Piotr Rawicz and his novel. *Engraved in Flesh* is the fruit of that hope.

A. R.

Moortown Farm, Devon 1992
Woodside Park, London 1993–6
Woodside Park, London 2007

Introduction to the Second Edition

Quite a few publishers (nameless in order to spare their blushes) read *Blood from the Sky* at my behest, were perceptive enough to agree with me that it is a masterpiece and made kind noises about my earliest essay on it. For what I understood were financial reasons, none of them felt able to reissue the novel, with or without a section of the essay as an introduction. So I decided to write the present book and, in 1996, published it ahead of an eventual republication of the 1964 translation of the novel. I own the rights to the translation outside the USA and Canada (having bought them from the original publisher, Secker and Warburg) and later revised and completed it. Although in general the translation was excellent, ten passages were omitted, as I explain in my text. I also corrected some of the religious and wartime terminology, revised a handful of stylistic infelicities and mistakes, and restored the historic present in a number of paragraphs.

In 2003, Yale University Press finally reissued the novel *in the unrevised translation*, with a specially written introduction by Lawrence Langer. That is the edition of the translation for sale in the USA and Canada. In 2004, Elliott and Thompson published my revised translation in the UK, with a preface explaining the circumstances of and reasons for the revision.

I also included an *Afterword* which is a distillation of *Engraved in Flesh* and of my entries on Rawicz in two reference books: *Jewish Writers of the 20th Century*, Sorrel Kerbel (ed.), Fitzroy Dearborn, New York and London, 2003 and *The Holocaust Novel*, Dictionary of Literary Biography, Volume 299, Efraim Sicher (ed.), Gale, Detroit 2004. The Elliott and Thompson edition is available everywhere outside the USA and Canada. I thank Mark Thwaite for reprinting the *Afterword* on his excellent website, www.readysteadybook.com.

Finally, thanks are due to Steven Jaron, for bibliographical and other advice during my preparation of the second edition of *Engraved in Flesh*. For this is not a mere reprint of the first edition. I have taken the opportunity to revisit my text, revise certain infelicities, correct detected errors, modify various statements, and update the bibliography. It is gratifying to note that, in the ten years between the two editions, more attention is being paid to Rawicz's great novel. I would like to think that my insistence on its significance and radical importance has played a small part in the changed atmosphere surrounding a neglected masterpiece.

Seven Thoughts

FOR PIOTR RAWICZ AND JAKOV LIND

Ideas are to objects as constellations are to stars.
Knowledge is open to question but truth is not.

Walter Benjamin

The most violent thought cannot move a single pebble.

Robert Antelme

Your mills of death grind the white flour of the promise.

Paul Celan

When the Temple was destroyed, the Messiah was born.

Midrash Lamentations, 2 (57)

All I can see is the Holy Nothingness which
gives life to the world.

Rav Shneur Zalman of Lyady, 1745–1813
(on his death-bed)

Circumcise
this one's word,
on this one's
good heart write
the living Nothing

Paul Celan

Whatever we forget is remembered somewhere.

Yom Kippur liturgy

1

The Hopeless Merry-Go-Round

When Dante's *Inferno* is realised on earth, when the tenor and vehicle of metaphor are conflated, then God, meaning and life are placed in the dock, in the courtroom where God himself may be pronounced mad. Literature, language and rhetoric are placed in the other dock, in that harbour whence the licence to set sail shall come at a high price, if at all. S. Szende, the last documented escapee from occupied Poland, witnessed in the L'wow ghetto children playing at '*aktions*': they divided themselves up into hunted Jews, Jewish ghetto police, Nazi SS officers and Ukrainian militants. A passing SS officer noticed that some details were wrong, and gave the children professional advice about how to improve their impersonations. Other children, in various camps, played at 'going to the gas chamber', surely the ultimate as-if situation – it is not only in artistic works that we find what Claude Lanzmann calls 'a fiction of reality'.

Fifty years after the Hitlerite death camps and concentration camps, we are free to walk along the partly reconstructed railway line at Birkenau in the opposite direction to the trains which took people to the *selektions* and the gas chambers, as if a symbolic gesture, whether on the ground – in the place that has become the symbol of genocide – or in a poem, might contribute to a useful reaction. We would like to think it could, even though of necessity the gesture rides on what Jean Améry calls 'the hopeless merry-go-round of figurative speech'. So serious are the issues, so high are the stakes, that we must acknowledge our virtual but not absolute helplessness, especially if God is indeed indicted as mad, steeped in his own vomit, as Piotr Rawicz's magnificently indirect, darkly humorous and deeply troubling book suggests. It is significant that the book is the last major Holocaust novel in English translation to be published in paperback, forty years after the hardback editions. For many years it was virtually ignored in the critical literature.[1]

We who come after, after the events and after the reading of the events by the most powerful participant observers[2] – Levi, Katsetnik 135633, Antelme, Rawicz himself, to name only four – and after the later remembrancers, notably Martin Gilbert in *Holocaust* and Claude Lanzmann in *Shoah*, we who come after can no longer even attempt the impossible and ideal or idealised objectivity that would protect us, hopelessly, against the charge of exploitation. Now we must embrace our deepest and most intimate fears of abandonment and loss. In the early years of the new millennium, serious people must acknowledge that with and after Auschwitz, Hiroshima and Nagasaki the world went to hell and remains there. AIDS and Chernobyl, man-made famine and mass murder, lethal climate change, deregulation and authoritarianism: we are no longer at home in our only world. This is, among other things, an ontological problem, not least for a new grandfather. *Blood from the Sky* – an early ontological reading of a twentieth century hell on earth – was written well over forty-five years ago.

Robert Antelme and Primo Levi show us how a man, a person, can remain a human being even when reduced to an apparent nothing. This is the world of Beckett, and behind him Dante and *Job*. Rawicz's Boris is a character in a novel and has a job to do, which is to conflate his reality as an end and his reality as a means, to exist over time, the time of our reading, to survive simultaneously the Nazis and the author's (let us say the narrator's) construction, while the author himself, his work done, is left free for the next twenty years to roam around Paris getting drunk, getting laid, having a good time while keeping the demons at bay, and generally being a bohemian until he blows his brains out after the death of his wife.[A] In other words we are assisting at a completely normal state of affairs. Rawicz wrote this book *as if* for life, maybe even without the *as if*. In the end, that is until the end and after the end, the life not the death is what counts – as with Primo Levi and Paul Celan. The real life generated one 'wantonly brilliant book',[3] which more than compensates for the version of Oblomov Rawicz cultivated as his persona. Having refused 'a heavenly mansion raging in the dark', Piotr's news may well have been, in the words of the same poem of Yeats, 'the night's remorse'.

Written for life, *Blood from the Sky* is not a mere allegory, Boris not a mere cypher – but, even so, we are not primarily in that traditional fictional territory where characters are understood in terms of the dialectic between socio-pathological and psycho-pathological explanatory structures, that territory where the mental and the material interact within the parameters of relative normality. This book is and cannot but be a picaresque philosophical poem in prose – 'prose is our poetry' indeed, in Franz Rosenzweig's words – in which Boris's ontological awareness is central to the process of writing and thus of our reading. The frame narrative includes poems, dialogues, digressions, *rallentandos*, footnotes, quotations and does its best at times to confuse our reading of the broken tale told by Boris, which begins with the German occupation of East Galicia, now Western Ukraine, in 1941. Boris knows that there is no hope at all for the Jews of occupied Europe – he knows this even before the occupation and the setting up of ghettos. He is aware of the deportations. The word has been abroad and come back.[4]

Blood from the Sky is not a book for the reader who likes a straightforward tale, nor is it for the squeamish. But even one reading of it changes the reader and the reader's perception of the world we have all inherited: against the small hope generated by Rawicz's having written the book at all, stands the large despair of the *Tremendum* (in Arthur Cohen's word),[5] that which we cannot comprehend, our minds on fire in the burning bush of a historical caesura which cannot be transcended, let alone redeemed. At the centre of Piotr's being, there was a black hole in a white night (this was a man, only more so). Yet, while death himself (in French, herself) may have at last felt remorse after Auschwitz, Piotr's suicide, like that of Levi, Borowski, Celan, Améry, Kosinski and others, should not over-obsess us.[B] As with Levi and Celan, a complex and unique combination of factors triggered the finger (literally in Piotr's case), when Piotr died by his own hand. Let us concentrate on the work of his life, the life of his work, be grateful for his gift to a world he rendered a little less unbearable precisely because he bore the burden, because he saw clearly, because he agreed 'to keep watch over absent meaning', in Blanchot's wonderful formulation.

Facts are events that really happened, but understood only through description, which can come in more than one version. Meaning in history, if there is any, is engendered by and through narrative. Piotr's literary narrative is at war with itself, deliberately so. The story of the main character, Boris, moves in and out of synch with its alleged provenance, the frame narrator's recording of Boris's conversations and writings. In a territory where metaphor is overwhelmed by reality, where documentation floods and suffocates through its ever-increasing weight, it is the architectonic structure of a complex literary work that bears the burden of personal necessity which is writing – in order that memory itself shall survive. The reader feels that the author has to persuade himself that it is worth the effort of remembering anything at all, let alone those chosen to be murdered. In this baroque phantasmagorical hallucinatory apocalyptic and metaphysical novel, Piotr Rawicz writes his reading (and we read his writing) of Nazi occupation before and during, inside and outside, the ghettos of Poland and East Galicia (though neither is named), prior to the final deportations to the camps. He himself was born in L'wow in the year that East Galicia became part of Poland after the collapse of the Austro-Hungarian Empire in the wake of World War One.[C] He reads/writes the events with black humour, surrealist disjunction, even blasphemy. He achieves his perspective by means of an extreme and radical 'distancing' or 'alienation' or 'defamiliarisation' (or however we translate the Russian Formalist term *ostraneniye)* which the history – a conflation of world history and personal history (Kafka's phrase 'the world history of the soul' comes to mind) – possessed by Rawicz required of him, both ethically and aesthetically. He is *as if* detached.[6] Sometimes the *as-if* persona of a constructed book is missed by critics, such as those who misread Primo Levi's own *as-if* construction, namely the conceptual framework of a scientific experiment, and mishear its *as-if* tone, that of a factory report.[7]

Rawicz's postscript beginning 'this is not a historical record' has been cited, by some readers, as a contradiction of the way the book is offered as a story drawn from a survivor's testimony.[8] But I would say that this conclusion summarises in an ironic way the book's ontological rejection of the possibility of objective historical *explanation.* The book purports to tell a story, even a true story, but this hardly makes it even a fictional historical record, despite its mediated links with the author's life – which I discuss in the present work from time to time. History deals with necessary conditions, not the sufficient conditions that might make sense of, for example, the gratuitous and extreme cruelty towards children so horrifyingly described by Rawicz.[9] To attempt a literary telling is not to avoid explanatory structures but it is to foreground the personal, the desperately personal, the personally desperate, while honouring the reader who will take on board (in the second dock referred to at the beginning of this essay?) the way of telling – the structural complexity itself being a holistic architectonic metaphor or translation. This yields a 'natural' progression and the conclusion is a natural mutation of the beginning; in other words the book dares tell not only the *Tremendum* but the *Tremendum* filtered through the mind of the main character, in this case an intellectual (intellectual disgust at the saloon bar), a lover (with Don Juan's libido and sense of responsibility), a poet (late symbolist excess), a Jew (whose Jewishness amounts to nothing more but also nothing less than an awareness of the destiny of his fellow Jews, whose faces, accent, or behavioural traits give them away to collaborators or Nazis occupiers sooner or later). This is an archetypical geometry of forces.

Rawicz wrote his book before the historical approach associated with Hayden White and his school, a narratological historicism, a meta-fictional historiography, that can enable a subjective or literary telling of indisputable factuality.[10] Boris's texts are, as it were, literature. The author's apparent detachment is the only objective correlative available to incarnate the terrible and unbearable reality – in the character's legitimate awareness, that is to say an awareness that is not predicated upon authorial hindsight – which is the reality of impending genocide. The white heat of his anger is silent, untold and unspoken as befits a process of mourning, but buried alive between the savagely lucid words of a wild joker, a trickster, a voice from the front line, alongside such writers as Katsetnik 135633, Jacques Presser and Jakov Lind. The deepest fear is that there is no meaning, certainly no redemptive meaning, left in the world. At best, writing shall generate a minimal counter-charge (' . . . in the heart's mouth / an awakened shibboleth', wrote Celan) to nothingness. History, specifically the Jewish history to which the key characters of Garin, Leo L. and Cohen relate themselves, is not a source of meaning, not a physic of memory, if I may adapt a phrase of Rosenstock-Huessy quoted by Yerushalmi.

Apparent detachment and indirection are enabled by means of the frame narrative technique: the author has a narrator[11] tell the story of the story of Boris, and this discourse is interspersed, sometimes seamlessly, with Boris's first-person and very singular account. Boris does not 'look Jewish', unlike so many of his traditional co-religionists in Ukraine and Poland. Furthermore he is rich, blond, aristocratic, sensitive, sexual, secularly intelligent – indeed one of the most hyper-intelligent and quick-witted characters in all literature – but also Jewishly aware. He speaks perfect Polish, Ukrainian and German, which along with his non-Jewish looks was a rare combination in the war, and these elements constitute the device which enables the novel to proceed as well as Boris to survive. But he is, naturally, that is to say covenantally, circumcised. The sign of the covenant is an inscription, an engraving in his very flesh. If discovered he will die, and die more horribly, because he will have fooled for a time even experts in identification of Jews, namely any Nazi worth his salt, the very salt literally rubbed into people's wounds on some occasions. In this respect and all other things being equal (whatever that may mean and which they weren't very often), it was by definition an advantage to be a woman. The absence of foreskin, that zero, is death. But the penis is life in the mind/body of a very sexual man which Boris – like his progenitor Rawicz – is, and it is what empowers his survival and his ability to write.

Death and life merge in the penis. God's covenant is a high-risk strategy, as Isaac knew, although, as Hyam Maccoby points out in his reading of the covenant in *The Sacred Executioner*, there is no suggestion that Isaac is spared by God because he had been circumcised. More important even than the account of the origin of circumcision in Genesis 17:9–12, is the mysterious but highly charged story in Exodus 4:24–6, of the wife of Moses, Zipporah, who circumcises her own son because Moses, her 'bridegroom of blood', has failed to do so. Maccoby's creative retranslation of the passage deserves careful consideration. As does Spinoza's remark, quoted in the commentary to Hertz's edition of the Pentateuch: 'Such great importance do I attach to the sign of the Covenant, that I am persuaded that it is sufficient by itself to maintain the separate existence of the nation for ever'. Thus Spinoza anticipates Gilles Deleuze.

Blood from the Sky is an early and rare masterpiece in what has become known as Holocaust fiction. Published in 1961 and contemporaneous with Wiesel's *Night* and Schwarz-Bart's *Last of the Just*, it appeared not long after the second edition of two profound and important non-fiction works, Primo Levi's *If This Is a Man* (1958, original edition 1947) and Robert Antelme's *L'Espèce humaine* (1957, original edition 1947), the two key books – with their echoing titles and publishing histories – of the first generation of publications, the latter translated only in 1992[12] under the title of *The Human Race* – a better translation might have been *Humankind*. Relative to the other great works in the literature under consideration, this masterpiece has been as neglected as Piotr's. It is, however, as essential, as quintessential indeed, as *If This Is a Man*, and that is the highest praise one can pay it. *La Douleur* by Antelme's wife Marguerite Duras, herself a writer of the greatest distinction but far more productive, can serve as a disturbing introduction to his one and only book.[18] As for *Blood from the Sky*, it was written directly in Rawicz's sixth language, French.[D] It is his only book-length work of fiction. His other published book, *Bloc-notes d'un contre-révolutionnaire*, an account of the 1968 May events, does not, I'm sure you will agree, go sufficiently against his own grain to generate the power and excitement of his novel.[E]

That one who saw himself and was seen by his friends and lovers as a contemporary version of Oblomov should tear out of his guts even one great book is material for thanksgiving. It is a matter of some interest that *Blood from the Sky* was 'too literary' for Primo Levi,[13] and indeed Levi's chasteness as a man and as a writer are at the opposite extreme to Piotr's world historical view of his own soul.[F] Cynicism, boredom, laziness, booze, cafe-haunting, sexual irresponsibility, poverty, *je m'en foutisme*, chaos, romantic idealism, all were present in the life of this survivor,[G] this 'capitaliste de la douleur' (his own self-description),[14] this graphomaniac who wrote thousands of fragments,[H] rising above or rather digging beneath his chaos just once to engender, organise, write and complete *Blood from the Sky*.

Life on the margin of death: if Ernie in Schwarz-Bart's *The Last of the Just* (a wonderful sibling book which cries out to be read 'against' *Blood from the Sky)* is a saint and a martyr, Boris from an equally distinguished line is a world-weary seducer and a poet, a cultivated but saloon bar intellectual and provincial philosopher given to flights of fancy. As a character in a novel, Boris is not obliged to be a great poet, a sublime philosopher: some readers ask too much. Boris is too busy, you see, his agenda is other. His writing career began precociously, preputially. At eight days old he was *written* into a community of fate. Without the *Shoah*, Boris would have spent his life between the bed and the desk and the cafe – in a big city somewhere in Ashkenazia, well to the east of Paris.[15] Sometime between the end of the war and the late fifties, Boris, whose vocation is to remember, finds time to write the lengthy text the narrator has to cut, you might say to circumcise. The penis is not only the pen, but the word too. The organ of God's covenant is the sign of life for the sexual man, the sign of death if he is caught, the palimpsest of life and death which is literary writing of this magnificence.

Blood from the Sky is a very early example of the self-referential post-modern novel, with desire, mind, writing, the body all merging, collapsing kaleidescopically. Note well: it is not solipsistic. It does not get up its own nose or any other orifice – thus relieving the reader of similar discomfort. It is necessarily self-referential because of its ontological preoccupations. Even in a world of putrefaction, cockroaches, bedbugs and rats, mind can transcend even a Boris's body (read prick), memory can salvage his town, his people.[11] This unworthy man is the vehicle of the metaphorical possibilities he disdains as useless – what use is comparison, the very root of understanding, when children are tortured before his eyes? Boris has to be a full-bodied, presence-minded character we believe in, or the covenantal mediation between the realism of destruction and the idealism of mental process would disintegrate into, at best, nothingness/*néant*, at worst, buzz/*frisson*.

Boris's tale is rooted not only in the lived history of his people but in their traditional modes of telling, in Hasidic stories and in bible. *Blood from the Sky* tracks the memory of *midrash* as do Katsetnik 135633, Potok, Wiesel, Jabès, Heimler. Katsetnik 135633, an ex wunderkind-rabbi, was 'not literary enough' for Primo Levi,[13] the exact opposite of Levi's view of Rawicz mentioned earlier. Rawicz himself, incidentally, told me he thought Katsetnik 135633 was 'hysterical, but authentically hysterical'. In Rawicz, this tracking of *midrash* is mediated through Gogol and Dostoevsky, Jarry and Lautréamont, Beckett and Camus, Artaud and Kafka (the last named himself a midrashic tracker of genius and whose breath-turning story, 'In the Penal Colony' tells of another engraving in the flesh), in other words the literary rather than the philosophical writers associated with French existentialism. *Blood from the Sky* in its own high modernist way is an expression of deep spirituality, the last gasp of a certain Polish Jewish symbiosis, which Rawicz himself saw slightly differently as being embodied in the work of the man he considered the greatest writer of our time, Adolf Rudnicki. Rudnicki, Rawicz insists in his introduction to Danilo Kiš's *Sablier* (*Hourglass*), evoked not only the destruction, but the 'object' destroyed. It was a symbiosis rich in possibility, desperately interesting, tragically defeated. In his introduction to Rudnicki's *Le Lion du Saint Sabbath*, Rawicz distinguishes his subject's approach from that of Bruno Schulz on the one hand (the matrix of whose stories is 'Jewish folklore and the Jewish spiritual landscape') and Lesmian and Tuwim on the other ('a judeity of the second degree as in Mandelstam or Pasternak'). The voice of Rawicz's narrator recalls Jean-Baptiste Clamance in Camus' *La Chute* (1956), and even more that of the narrator in Louis-René Des Forêts' *Le Bavard* (1946), a great book that is almost as neglected outside France as Antelme's *The Human Race*, and one which influenced Camus's own masterpiece.

The book keeps us in mind. Boris processes 'typical' events of the Occupation. The narrative is mental, the world the book invokes is mental too, in the sense that has returned after a couple of generations. It is a fable, the story fabulous. If the characters are patent puppets on the strings of a frame narrator himself pulled by the strings (talk about the anxiety of influence) of Rawicz, we are not bothered, as the book builds up to its climax: the inscription, the writing, the symbol in the very body of the main character whose prick is life, whose prick is death. Whose prick is destiny (Peter Wiles translates *queue* as 'tool' which gives him a pun in English).

The Ukraine of the novel is no Ukraine of the earth. It is a legendary Ukraine, a Jewish Ukraine of Hasidism and the *shtetl*, out of which mutated this particular Jew, with this particular combination of qualities that allow the story to develop at all, the story of occupation, ghetto, flight through Poland, prison and eventual freedom, as we know from the *incipit* of the book. All these are discussed in detail in Section 2 of this essay. There are clear hints in the book, for example in the Coda, that Boris is deported to Auschwitz ('the story of the tool had repercussions in the Great Plain of the Birches': for 'birches' read 'Birkenau') but we are spared the telling of this critical experience – which is the other zero, the other absence in the book. Some of Rawicz's own experiences in Auschwitz have been displaced in the novel to the pre-Auschwitz period of his life.[K] Any extravagance in this literally preposterous book is found, properly, in its structure. Rawicz is sparing in his descriptions of horror, both in what is included and by excluding Auschwitz. You cannot play down the horror as such e.g. – *ad absurdum* – have the German put out *one* eye of the child to reduce the horror by fifty per cent, but if you want to tell it in such a way as to avoid the reader's rejection/ denial (honourable but pointless) on the one hand and avoid toleration / assimilation (pointed but dishonourable) on the other, you have to 'alienate' the reader, and use your literary devices to prevent a fixation, a fetishisation, an over-focussing on the image. And so technique is ethical.

Blood from the Sky is a baroque pot-pourri of a book; a book of death and torture and murder, a cemetery of a cemetery (as he writes of one graveyard in which people were murdered); a blackly humorous book of the most extreme and powerful kind[16] by an author who tells the narrator who tells Boris (who is also Yuri) who tells the minor character the stoker whose journal is plagiarised after the war; a vortex of a book, a gyre of a book, and for what purpose? *To think atrocity, to enable the thinking of atrocity,* to distance it and thus bring us closer to evil and to madness, to the evil of individual people especially Nazis, to the (apparent?) madness of God, to the madness of ourselves. It represents the thinking of extremity by the process and enactment of remembrance. Not understanding, but storing up, and then remembering, and then shaping the remembrance. For this, Boris, a human litmus test for the worst of Europe, is put through the mill. The unspeakable is spoken, the unbearable is borne, through the book's rhetorical complexity, its architectonic constructedness. The tone is singular, as you will find when, for example, you read the terrible scenes of eye-gouging and tongue-cutting of children, or when men are buried up to their necks and pissed on. Rawicz writes as if through a Medusa's mirror lightly, at an angle both to the tone and colour of say Kosinski or Katsetnik 135633 on the one hand (Rawicz, incidentally, told me he got Kosinski to admit he was Jewish), and Levi or Antelme on the other. The darkest moments are not as chastely presented as in the latter, but not as lingered on as in the former. Rawicz found his own way, in one book only, of forcing our attention, through negative epiphanies, on how insufficient necessary conditions of explanation are. Reality is 'subscended', in Arthur Cohen's sense of the term.

Boris outwits the enemy. The enemy, in real life, was not the Germans in general, nor even 'the Nazis' as a group whose crimes can be 'explained' or even explained by historians of various tendencies like Christopher Browning or Raoul Hillberg (the latter a key participant in Lanzmann's film *Shoah*), but men and women each of whom made a choice. At any given moment, the gratuitous killing of, for example, a child, happened because a human being chose to behave in an inhuman way. We must insist that it was *individuals* who killed *individuals* even under a daemonic system – fed by antisemitic ideology — whose very *essence* was torture, symbolised by the crucifixion of Captain Wolf,[17] and whose aim was the industrial murder of millions.

The necessary conditions may be collective, but the sufficient conditions pertain to the individual murderer and also, though differently, to the individual victim, whose regular degradation and occasional corruption must not, where appropriate, be glossed over, but which must be measured according to a different calculus than the torturer's.[18] Rawicz's anger is displaced and projected onto a character whose survival gives us a homeopathic dose of hope that intelligence, at least, is worth cultivating, for without that Boris would die and along with him the incarnation of historical memory, buried alive, briefly stirring the soil of a far field, when the weather insists.

Blood from the Sky, not a historical record, not an autobiography, is redolent of the atmosphere of the time, conjures the mood and feel of the killing fields. And, in truth, on rereading it, I ask myself if the book is not as 'detached' as it might be thought or felt to be on first reading, and as we might need to think and feel it. It exploits the metaphysics and symbolism spoken and written by Boris, to guide us prismatically, by the 'bright light of shipwreck' (Oppen) through the nightmares experienced in the ghetto, in flight, in prison and in freedom. The six great set-piece tableaux (described in Section 2 of this essay), namely the death of Leo (Chapter 5), the liquidation of the hospital (Chapter 13), the cruelty to children in the workshops (Chapter 18), the soldiers pissing on men buried up to their necks (Chapter 19), Boris's killing of the Pole (Chapter 20), Boris's disputation with the Ukrainian (Chapter 33), all are quite fantastical, theatrical, visionary in their colour and their strength, but restrained, held in check and balanced by or against the 'alienation', in both senses, of Boris, that is by the control of the author, ironic and eirenic to an extreme degree; at the same time, it is as if the book was dictated in a waking dream.

The terrible beauty of these scenes, in particular those involving Leo (the Judenrat), Garin (the workshops) and Cohen (the hospital) in which all the dams of hopeless hope are flooded, their power and their hurt, are so extreme that they can only be viewed through a hallucinatory prism, a prism of words which reflect and deviate the darkness, and these words belong to all of us. The writer does not, need not, cannot give a linear account of his data, for this presupposes a model of reality which is always highly misleading, not least in circumstances where the power of the enemy was virtually absolute and controlled the modalities of discourse as lived by everybody. The perpetrators understood that it is easier to destroy the body after you have first destroyed the spirit. On the other hand, individual freedom and honour could often only be bought at the price of a cruel death, such as Boris only just avoids, and avoids certainly not because of his virtues, unless intelligence be a virtue, which we may think it is, though we might not want to call it, in Adorno's phrase, a 'moral category'. There is a sense in which Boris, like some of Arnost Lustig's characters, is free, but he is free only on the margin of the absolute – Nazi power over Jews – while the author constructs a virtual reality in words which shape a horror Boris must keep at arm's or rather mind's length.

Boris's apparent nihilism is shadowed by an armature of self-expression not derived from the suffering itself. After all, he comes to this situation with a pre-existing world view: even his desperate state of affairs is not as extreme as the Auschwitz described by Levi and Améry, the Janowska described by Wells and Drix, the Treblinka desribed by Stiffel, the Belzec described by Reder (as told by Gilbert), the Gandersheim described by Antelme in his merciless and exemplary micro-phenomenology of servitude transcended. Boris will live, says an astrologer, because he does not deserve to die. Only a cosmic catastrophe on this scale could shock a man such as Boris – for whom the world is anyway putrefying and doomed to entropy – into working to stay alive. Even Boris learns there is more to life than philosophical disgust, more to life than sexual love, for example his responsibility to survive despite the high risk of a fated death as a result of the self-same sexual organ: the conscience of prick becomes the prick of conscience. He too belongs. He shall be part of the remnant: 'Israel lives' rather than 'perish Judah'. He too will fight to survive, as you do (or sometimes don't), like Camus' Rieux, like Vladimir and Estragon. Given where Boris comes from in terms of attitude, given the world history of his soul, his commitment to remember – which becomes his truth, his passion – is all the more remarkable.

The dialectical tension in the novel resides in the counterpoint, within the frame narrative and thus already dialectical, between one man's apparently irrelevant banalities of poem and philosophy and the extraordinary confrontations of degraded victims and differently degraded killers during the collapse of ghetto institutions, their death rattle, the implosion of the delusive hope they offered. Boris must flee with Naomi (and put up with being faithful to her since sexual adventures would be too dangerous), protected by his linguistic talents, his non-Jewish appearance, his passivity which is a kind of innocence, his passion for remembrance. Rawicz, through the manic energy of his inventiveness, belies his real life persona of Oblomov, draws the opposites together, ties the knot of art, fixes the explosion, constructs an artefact of the most savage and convulsive beauty.

Remembrance not understanding is the key. Nothing in Boris's existential philosophy or symbolist poetry equips him to understand, but native intelligence at last demands that he remember, that he witness, that he carry his community's past into a future on paper if not in life. For this he must keep going even in the lowest depths, the prison cells of Part Three of the novel. To 'understand' would probably have killed him by miring him in an unequal battle where the enemy holds all the cards (except the joker), for the tools of understanding then as now are utterly inadequate to the task. Boris is an ancient mariner, like Rawicz himself. If genocide is the central issue for ontology, the ultimate problematic of theodicy, then given their answers the world is inherently damned.[19] A novel such as this cannot give meaning to a crazy universe but it can render the absence of meaning less meaningless, not least for Piotr himself with his great ontological lament, his eschatological keening from the terrestrial inferno ('in great poetry, when is it not a question of last things?' wrote Celan of Mandelstam, but it also applies to Celan himself and to the handful of other great writers of the Holocaust such as Rawicz: if you know, you can speak).[20] And what is true of writing is even truer of love which, as Rawicz tells us in *Bloc-notes*, is what God made the world out of. Piotr, like Boris, came back from the dead, with a return ticket for his transport. This Orpheus was his own Eurydice.

Notes to 'The Hopeless Merry-Go-Round'

1 See the Introduction on page 9 and the Commented Bibliography for more details of the two paperback editions and the revisions I made for the UK edition. The book first appeared in hardback in the UK from Secker and Warburg in 1964 and in the United States in the same year from Harcourt, Brace and World. It was translated by Peter Wiles (see acknowledgments). A few brief passages in the French are missing from the original English translation, to the surprise of Mr Wiles (letter dated 26 March 1993), and although I have restored them in my revised translation, I have retained a (revised) Appendix about them in this second edition of *Engraved in Flesh* for the benefit of American and Canadian readers. Peter Wiles also persuaded me that *The Blood of Heaven* would not necessarily be an improvement on *Blood from the Sky* as a translation of the title: *Le Sang du ciel.* In a decidedly peculiar interview with Nicole Dethoor, Rawicz states that he wanted to call the whole book by the title of the first section, *The Tool and the Art of Comparison*, but Gallimard demurred, supposedly for commercial reasons. Helen Wolff, the legendary expatriate publisher who brought the book to her associate publisher Harcourt Brace, wrote to me in 1982, after the death of Rawicz, that she felt it was 'the only work which totally transmutes the actual events into a kind of dark poetry'. She continued: 'It is a dismal commentary on present-day publishing that exceptional quality militates against a book'. And that was in 1982. We were both lamenting the sad fact that nobody wanted to risk a soft-cover edition. The original edition of *Le Sang du ciel* was published by Gallimard in 1961 and reissued in 1982 after Piotr's death. It is undoubtedly a disconcerting, even a scandalous book, and its long neglect too was disconcerting and scandalous. But as Primo Levi writes in his preface to Jacques Presser's *The Night of the Girondists:* 'scandals are good: they provoke discussion and make for inner clarity'.

2 *The Janowska Road* by Wells, which Rawicz often mentioned to me and to other friends, is a most important and exemplary act of witness. But apart from one or two articles and a later

autobiography, it is the only piece of writing by its author. It is, in the words of Rawicz in his preface to *Sablier* (*Hourglass*) by Danilo Kiš, one of the key 'hurlements articulés' (articulated howls) written without any 'procédé littéraire' (literary process). Apart from Wells, other single and singular texts of similar importance have been written by Leon Thorne, Max Perkal, Henry Herzog, Elisabeth Sommer Lefkovits, Samuel Drix, Jean Samuel (Primo Levi's Pikolo), Chaim Kaplan and many others. The early masterpieces by writers who do deploy 'procédé littéraire' are hard acts for themselves to follow – on and off the page – as the lives and/or works of, for example, Wiesel, Kosinski, Levi, Schwarz-Bart, Antelme, Begley and Lind, reveal, in their very different ways. For example, Levi's survival was in part due to his being a writer in the first place (see my little book on him), and *If This Is a Man*, a complex literary artefact, reflects this. As for Rawicz himself, given the full blown literary brilliance of his great work, we may well wonder what, if anything, he would have produced, apart from *Bloc-notes*, had he lived. Or take one of the books by Kosinski written after his only masterpiece, *The Painted Bird*, namely *The Hermit of 69th Street*, with a sexual innuendo in the very title, and with the narrator's footnotes on virtually everyone of the six hundred pages, quoting among others a certain Kosinski and many of his acquaintances (though not, unfortunately, Rawicz). Piotr would have been deeply intrigued by *The Hermit* . . . and would doubtless have written a learned and entertaining review in *Le Monde*. Recent revelations concerning Kosinski suggest that he was not a 'participant observer' but invented several of the episodes in *The Painted Bird* which he always claimed he had witnessed or experienced. But as Louis Begley in his review of a biography of Kosinski – the book oddly does not mention Rawicz – rightly says, this does not make *The Painted Bird* less wonderful. On the contrary.

3 The phrase, a blurb writer's dream, is Irving Howe's. It comes from his important general essay *Writing and the Holocaust* in the eponymous collection edited by Berel Lang. Theodore Solotaroff in his collection of essays, *The Red Hot Vacuum*, includes a brief and valuable article, and A. Alvarez reprints in *Beyond all this Fiddle* his percipient review of a number of

Holocaust novels, including Piotr's; Elie Wiesel's review in *The New Leader* is as interesting for what it does not say as for what it does, as is Dayan Rosenman's article. Wiesel freely admitted to me that his attitude to sexuality differed completely from that of Rawicz. The Gallimard file of reviews is quite large. Of particular interest are the ones by Maurice Nadeau, Jean-Bloch Michel and Jacqueline Piatier. *L'Arche* published a strange and edgy interview with Rawicz by Anna Langfus, herself a Holocaust writer of distinction, in which a complete non-meeting of minds ended in a trading of insults. In Frank Stiffel's powerful book on the Warsaw Ghetto, Treblinka and Auschwitz, *The Tale of the Ring: a Kaddish*, we find Piotr himself making a ghost-like appearance in a Cracow park and later standing beside Stiffel in the urinals of the medical block in Auschwitz. We also find Piotr in a story by Danilo Kiš (see elsewhere in this book) and a novel by Luba Jurgenson. In a more recent novel by Ana Novac, our mutual friend is enabled to speak at length. The cover of the original UK edition of *Blood from the Sky*, published by Secker and Warburg, contains a puff by Angus Wilson: 'It is fierce in its impact, unusual and often horrifyingly funny'. It is no longer possible to discover whether Wilson's comment was extracted from a longer text. According to his biographer, Margaret Drabble, he often wrote cover comments for Secker and Warburg.

4 See Geoffrey Hill's poem 'Annunciations'.

5 See Cohen's powerful and suggestive theological reading of the Holocaust: *The Tremendum*. After settling on 'Churban' when writing about Levi rather than 'Shoah' or 'Holocaust', I now think 'Tremendum' could be the most appropriate word – but it won't be taken up. See also Rabbi Albert Friedlander's article, 'The Misuses of the Holocaust'. Claude Lanzmann, however, *prefers* the word 'Holocaust' – see his *London Magazine* interview. Concerning the Holocaust as historical caesura: Rawicz, in his introduction to Kiš's *Sablier* (*Hourglass*), dismisses Adorno and the famous remark about poetry after Auschwitz by drawing readers' attention to the traditional Jewish theological view that catastrophe, even the supreme catastrophe, is *not* historical caesura, that the Holocaust 'constitutes a new edition, a

repetition of an archetypal and metahistorical event: the destruction of the temple in Jerusalem' and that Jeremiah 'treated this event in the language of poetry'. What and where would art be, Rawicz asks, without human suffering? What and where indeed, but this does not answer the theological question, nor does it tell us what Rawicz's views were, though we may be tempted to suppose that he agreed with the traditional view.

6 'The *epistemic* objectivity of method does not preclude *ontological* subjectivity of subject matter' (John Searle).

7 I would now want to reword slightly what I wrote on page thirteen of my book on Levi because of a possible confusion between Levi's perception of the camps, and that of the Nazis. It is clear from *If This Is a Man* that Levi is not saying that the Nazis themselves saw the camp as a scientific experiment.

8 Including several reviewers, and Jacqueline Rose herself in passing in her book on Sylvia Plath. The note to the reader at the end of Philip Roth's *Operation Shylock* ending 'This confession is false' bears a passing resemblance to Rawicz's post-script. Irrespective of possible influence, it would be of interest to learn if Roth has read *Blood from the Sky*.

9 See the Lanzmann interview for more on the question of necessary and sufficient conditions.

10 See White's essay 'The Historical Text as Literary Artefact' in *The Writing of History: Literary Form and Historical Understanding*, the essay by Lionel Cossman in the same book, and other books by White. Gertrude Himmelfarb has attempted a refutation. Not without interest, it goes too far.

11 See Section 2 *passim*.

12 See also Note F in Section 3 of this essay and my essay on Antelme and Levi and Améry, mentioned there. See too Note 18 below.

13 See my *At an Uncertain Hour: Primo Levi's War against Oblivion* for this and other references to Levi throughout *Engraved in Flesh*. I gave my second copy of *Le Sang du ciel* to Levi. Levi's wife is certain he never wrote about the book in some [as yet untranslated] *feuilleton*.

14 This is an amusing, touching, ironical and self-mocking description (see also Note E in Section 3 of this essay), obviously alluding to Paul Eluard's early book *Capitale de la douleur*

(published in 1926), though the pun is Rawicz's, not Eluard's. In 1926, the poet was a member of the earliest inner circle of the Surrealist movement. He and Breton applied to join the Communist Party at the end of that year. They were expelled in 1933. In a famous lecture, 'Poetic Evidence', given in London in 1936, Eluard said: 'In 1925, at the time of the Moroccan war, Max Ernst upheld with me the watchword of fraternisation of the French Communist Party'. Eluard rejoined the Communist Party in 1942. There is much in *Blood from the Sky* that would please the surrealists. The May Events, about which more elsewhere (see again Note E in Section 3 as well as the note in the bibliography on Rawicz's review of Witkiewicz), owed as much to the spirit of surrealism as to socialism.

15 Clive Sinclair's fictional European Jewish diaspora state.

16 Auschwitz, one of the event-horizons (to use a term from astronomy) of the modern world, was indeed a cosmic catastrophe for humanity, certainly for those who have the possibility to worry about such matters. After such history, what is a life for? Answering that question brings different examples – in some remarkable cases – of affirmation. Antelme insists that you name yourself simply man or woman (see Note 18 below). Fackenheim insists you name yourself in your collective particularity, his eleventh commandment being 'no posthumous victories for Hitler', but even this admirable sentiment raises problems for human freedom. Jakov Lind's answer raises troubling issues which must await another essay. See also M. A. Bernstein on Fackenheim.

17 See the brief account in Nina Sutton's important biography of Bruno Bettelheim, citing the book by Thalmann and Feinermann.

18 While we have all learned from Levi's *The Drowned and the Saved* to maintain the ontological distinction between the victim and the murderer, nonetheless if we can impute responsibility to, for example, the SS it is precisely because – as Antelme insists – we are members of the same species as the perpetrators. Antelme: 'They have been able to dispossess us of everything save what we are'. 'It is because we are men like them that the SS are finally powerless before us'. 'The SS are only men, like us'. 'The executioner can kill a man but he cannot change him into

something else'. Back in 1947, Antelme took all that was best in anthropology, Marxism, phenomenology and existentialism, that is to say in himself as a man of his time, and wrote himself out of a cruel ordeal that should have killed him (see *La Douleur* for his wife's definitive account of the literal shape he was in after being rescued by François Mitterrand from Dachau, where he had ended up), wrote himself – through a relentless and continuing knowledge of freedom and death – into the rest of his life. He would not produce another book, but *The Human Race* stands with *If This Is a Man*, its exact contemporary, as the supreme non-fiction masterpiece in the literature of the camps, in his case Buchenwald and Gandersheim (a forced labour Kommando affiliated to Buchenwald). See also Ronald Aronson's *The Dialectics of Disaster* and *After Marxism* on evil, madness and genocide.

19 If this is not true the world, i.e. the great powers, would have mandated the United Nations to prevent or at least mitigate criminal tragedies like East Timor, Cambodia, Rwanda and Sudan. See my brief discussion of the Gulf War in a postscript note to *Wine from Two Glasses.*

20 *Those who know don't speak / Those who speak don't know* (Czeslaw Milosz)

2

The Vocation of the Witness

The story of the novel, a running commentary with notes, some key quotes

PART ONE OF THE NOVEL

The Tool and the Art of Comparison

The ghetto, its aura of false hope, leading to the death of the ghetto and its inhabitants, along with the death of hope.

The novel opens with the narrator in a Paris café, making bizarre comparisons. The customer is 'merchandise', the story is a 'shop' and then it becomes 'the tale of the tool or the art of comparison'. The narrator makes a sexual innuendo and recites a short poem. If we find ourselves thinking we have entered a mad world, Ionesco will come to mind; Dostoevsky. But we may prefer to say unreal rather than mad. Boris, the customer, makes his appearance. He is a survivor, a knowledge we retain as we travel through the book with him. This world is unreal because the author has inscribed us, the readers, in his book. This is *a writing*, and could not be more self-conscious. Rawicz exploits technique, not theme. His business is not, to quote a famous phrase, '*shoah* business'. Boris witnesses, the narrator writes. The problem of representation is faced from the very first page. The chapter ends with the first phoney footnote – which precedes the first flashback.

Chapter 2 flashes the reader back to the inhabitants of Boris's town, ordered to line up in the main square for deportation. One day, Boris's composition (sorry for the 'vulgar pun') will be 'on the subject of decomposition'. He admires some girls and discusses a poem he has not been writing, but we remember he is a character in a novel so the non-writing, written convincingly, matters not. Cruelly – and the novel wants us to know that Boris is not a likeable man – he tells a hunchbacked old rabbi to get false papers and try to pass for a non-Jew.

Chapter 3 tells his telling of what happened to the inhabitants of another town. He presents his hidden mistress with a wonderful gift, a splendid asset: a phial of cyanide . . . [1]

In Chapter 4, Boris proceeds to recount his crazy, plagiarised and pretentious theories – which reinforce rather than undermine his credibility with the careful reader – as well as some stories from his past, including 'on the one hand, my wanderings in neglected graveyards and through stretches of waste grounds, my peregrinations *ad limina* and the weeks that I spent at the court of some saintly miracle worker; on the other hand there were the days of debauchery, which to me was the sole possible expression of the sacred'. Chaste, Boris is not. Then, he tells of Leo, lawyer, hedonist and theatre lover – who could have left for a professorship at Harvard before the war and who compares himself to the head of the sacred Jewish community in Frankfurt at the time of the Black Death: Leo will shortly be appointed head of the Jewish Council, king of the ghetto, and who will have to make the *selektion* for the Nazis.[2] Rawicz incorporates the theme of the Jewish police in the ghetto, and indicts them. The leitmotif of putrefaction comes in (as we know, the Jews were vermin according to Nazi ideology), and the author relates it to the Holocaust. Sexual imagery proliferates, and this too is related to the Holocaust. Boris and Naomi are going to leave. Leo predicts they will become strangers to themselves but they must be witnesses: 'what matters is the integrity of the witnesses'.

Chapter 5. The author re-introduces the narrator in Paris. He asks Boris how Leo died. Boris heard it from someone else and builds in a clarification of the novel's chronological structure for our benefit. The death scene in which Leo is humiliated after he has given his wife their only cyanide pill – even though he loathes her (see Chapter 4) – and after his twelve councillors are hanged, darkly parodies religious carnival and generates theatre worthy of a Goya, a Bunuel.[3] The chapter ends with a long footnote in which Boris, at a later date, reflects on the episode and its consequences for our judgment. The footnote, one of several in the book, is another device, an architectonic trope, to distance, to contain, and to bring us back by the slowest route to the main road of the narrative.

There is more philosophical reflection in Chapter 6, and then we are taken back several months before Boris's departure. He reflects on Jewish history – on Shabbetai Zvi,[4] on Jacob Frank[5] and on the golem, which can be characterised as a *sitra akhra*[6] of the Messiah. Boris, we understand, is a man who thinks, who makes comparisons, or did. He tells us about Garin,[2] a rich and 'pitiless salesman travelling in false hopes', and explicitly described as a false Messiah who, supposedly, will save lives by means of his workshops, set up thanks to his wealth and influence. He is, like Leo, a classic figure from the ghetto archives which have finally begun to be published in the years since this novel was written. People clutch at straws, in order not to confront the truth. Do we blame them? The self-deceptions of the majority are a key theme in the book. Boris himself, who has recently seduced the virgin Naomi, is undeceived, and protected by his passivity, his cynicism, his hedonism, his nihilism, his detachment, but these are unconsciously guaranteed by his non-Jewish appearance, which guarantee is not worth the paper it is not written on, since what is written is itself ultimately linked to a zero, namely his foreskin, whose absence is always at mortal risk of being noticed and commented on. *Aktions* are expected. Leo's men will select from Garin's workshops. Rawicz milks the situation for the humour. What Leo says is grotesque, but everyone friend or foe is grotesque. Death and dying have been normalised.

Chapter 7 has 'a poison-vendor, formerly a chemist' offering the easy way out: 'here we have a very special mixture. I call it a *millefeuille*. It's as sweet-tasting as the honey-cake my mother used to bake for the festival of Purim'.[7] A conversation between a scholar Hillel and a poet Isaac gets nowhere fast. Senator Gordon reminds us of Janusz Korczak.[8]

In Chapter 8 Boris has a surreal conversation in the cemetery with the caretaker, concerning the latest arrivals, who were important people. 'Fifty eight suicides last night alone . . . Tarnovsky the poet. Hanged himself. Just look at that bruise. He had no money for poison'. Boris remembers Tarnovsky's translations and the bridge he had sought 'to throw across the Bosphorus, linking Mount Olympus and Mount Zion'. And then Boris recognises a corpse: one of his lovers, with a name as redolent as Naomi's: Shulamith.[9] In a powerful paragraph he recalls the night when they both lost their virginity. He wants to touch her but the caretaker does not allow it for religious reasons: Boris is a 'Cohen', a member of the priestly caste, forbidden by religious law to touch corpses.[10] He sees slave labourers demolishing tombstones. 'An *aleph* would go flying off to the left . . . a *gimel* would bite the dust . . . several examples of *shin* had just been smashed . . . Was the secret life of these murdered tombstones going to continue in these chips and granules?' This scene is parallelled in *The Last of the Just.* I myself saw in my grandfather's town in East Galicia a road paved by Jewish slave labour with tombstones from the old cemetery.[11] Boris understands he must leave before he too becomes one of the slaves. Death is no more sacred than life. Boris has to survive to remember the old cemetery. The holy letters will find a home in memory, in a book, which is the death of death.

In Chapter 9, jokes about soap made from human flesh circulate. Boris's ontological attitude to women is elaborated. He is rightly told by old Lena, a wise crone: 'It isn't you who are exceptional but your destiny' and 'the Town will become a thorn in your flesh. Inside . . . the town will be reborn' – a hint that he shall witness to the past, that is to say, write it, his town – including the cemetery, as told in the previous chapter. He looks through Lena's window and the past of his town unfolds. Lena predicts he will and must suffer greatly, but he will leave and survive because he hasn't earned the right to stay. Critically and conveniently (this is a novel), he finds the birth certificate of a Ukrainian Christian. Maybe he'll be able to sell it . . .

Chapter 10. The theme of torture is announced in a conversation with the narrator.

Chapter 11. All Goldbergs have to report to the main gate. Never to be seen again. A Nazi has been infected with gonorrhoea by a Goldberg. Or, asks a footnote, was it a Goldstein . . . Note the use of a footnote, a throwaway, to defocus the full horror of the mistake – yet we know it makes no difference anyway. The Goldsteins too will die in Belzec or Auschwitz.

The action moves forward in Chapter 12. There will be an *aktion*. The 'safe' workshops are to be emptied while Boris, in his 'safe' house, must leave with Naomi. The landlady guesses their truth. 'The question of the tool was taking on the colour of reality'. They leave and Boris recounts the classic story of a great rabbi who upbraids God, a projection of his own inherited sense of betrayal. Boris and Naomi hide in a well accompanied by rats. Boris, cruelly, tells Naomi about that zoological freak, the king rat, and relates it to the condition of his community.

Chapter 13. Semblance of reality; reality of semblance. The living of a lie is described in one of the great set pieces of the book: the hospital. There is no hope. Piotr Rawicz piles on the agony. The hospital is temporarily immune, being useful for the medical problems of the lady friends of the police and guards. Boris tells of the destiny of a perfect and 'superhuman' nurse (distress), of a stoker (genius) and of the superintendent (power). He makes love to the nurse Tamara a few times, their relationship suffused with 'earnest indifference, ironic tenderness'. The journal of David the stoker is quoted, the journal within the journal of Boris: the stoker's bliss is masturbation. He is happy when his father is deported and he attempts to drive his mother mad. In exchange for two cigarettes he acquires the amputated stump of his old teacher, 'a wonderful toy'. After the war, Boris tells the narrator, the journal was plagiarised by a caretaker who has murdered David.

Chapter 14 is full of irony and indirection. We know what will happen, where the patients will be sent. Cohen, the head doctor speaks, and reminds us that the prophet Elisha was bald too. Cohen defends the arithmetical approach to survival. Today he saved six hundred and seventy nine people and yielded up five hundred and sixty one. Even the hospital is not safe. It must be emptied. Nothing could have been done to prevent this. Everyone is on the margin, from the king of the ghetto to the humblest shithouse cleaner – Boris's own job in prison later on in the book, as it turns out. Death, slow or quick, now or later, these are the only choices, as Mordechai Anielewicz[12] knew, as Korcak[8] himself knew, as Ernie Levy in *The Last of the Just* knew. Chance meant that Emanuel Ringelblum and Chaim Kaplan died, that Piotr Rawicz and Eugene Heimler survived.

Chapter 15. Back to the narrator; a poem; a dialogue.

In Chapter 16, there are some extracts in verse and in prose from the journal of Boris. He discusses suicide and language, and quotes Leo: *la vertu du témoin*, the vocation or quality of the witness. Exiled in Paris, Boris, 'the "I" who had lived through the walled up town and all the rest' and survived 'Birch tree Walk' (ie Birkenau), reflects on literature: 'anti-dignity exalted to a system'; 'the art of rummaging in vomit' But 'one has to write', even though ' "the literary manner" or "literary process" ('procédé littéraire' – a phrase he will use twenty years later in his introduction to Kiš's *Sablier)* is an obscenity by definition'. The writer is compared to an insect, 'dissecting the world into tiny bits'; 'hardships will no longer slip through the nets of enumeration'. A critically important post-*Tremendum*[13] aesthetic is adumbrated in this chapter[14] and the following one.

In Chapter 17, the narrator tells us about the papers of Boris, how he selects from them, and this bears on our understanding of Boris's tale. The narrator explains that he has to be ruthless, removing the gibberish and the pseudo-lyrical. Some readers feel that this describes some of what remains even after the sifting and that this diminishes the book, but I argue that whether what remains is gibberish or is not gibberish does not matter. What matters is that Boris is a plausible character and that his writings reinforce his destiny in and through the discourse, which is to bear the burden of remembrance, not through his being a saintly rabbi, a holy fool, a pure boy, but through what he is: a sort of poet, a kind of philosopher, a classic womaniser, a Jew who can pass for a non-Jew even in the most unpropitious circumstances for such a pose, who will return to eventual life and freedom and the continuation of his old ways as a result of a magisterial and spontaneous leap of intelligence at the moment of truth. Of course he will never write a novel. His life is his novel, his sentimental education, so to speak. The narrator virtually apologises for what is to come: the horror, the horror. And the foregrounding of the process of writing here and elsewhere – cutting, editing etc – allows Rawicz to play down the horrors, permitting the reader to take them on board without a vicarious *frisson*.

We return to Boris in Chapter 18, and his account of the workshops, how the workers are played with by their tormentors, their hopeless situation, their self-deception, the fantasy of Garin. And 'there was a contractual obligation: those who lived would have to remember'. Forty children are shepherded into a cellar: a little girl, eight years old and hunchbacked, asks Boris: 'When our bodies rise from the dead, little uncle, as the holy scriptures say they will, shall I still have a crooked back?' Some soldiers find the cellar by accident. A little boy sticks out his tongue. They cut it out. The eyes of a little girl are gouged out. Boris is passive, even collusive. If he weren't, he would be killed: memory and the book would end. At this point I think of Améry, of Antelme, of Levi, of all the accounts one has read, and I bless Piotr for his courage in addressing the problem of complicity.[15] God then faints, surrounded by his own vomit. 'Two hours later Boris returns to the same spot, together with a nurse armed with a syringe. Several mutilated children were still suffering. The nurse went around distributing death, like portions of gingerbread stuffed with darkness', as Adina Szwajger[16] did in the Warsaw Ghetto. The image of gingerbread is breath-turning (in Celan's word) and serves as a weighty counter to the 'decomposition' of the book, which continually threatens to overwhelm its 'composition'. Remember Chapter 16: literature as anti-dignity, rummaging in vomit; the cockroaches referred to when Boris is imprisoned later. Can Boris tell it? Can Rawicz? The stoker David's narrative in Chapter 13, the soldier's words in Chapter 19: other narratives circulating within and around that of Boris have an uncertain destiny in this book. Finally, despite his proper revulsion from traditional comparison, despite his ambition to kill comparison – comparison after all could kill Boris in Chapter 33 – Rawicz offers us the terrible gift of an image from childhood; perhaps the dead children deserve it, perhaps the little girl will return in messianic days without her hunchback. We ourselves, as writers and readers, must take care to deserve the gift, and this requires us to read Rawicz's book as carefully as possible.

PART TWO OF THE NOVEL

The Journey

Flight, torture, killing, betrayals, flight, flight.

Chapter 19. They leave the hometown. Boris hears a partisan song whistled. 'The partisans murdered us, just as those whom they were fighting did'. Boris rehearses his *echt* Ukrainian nationality, and nationalism. He is now Yuri Goletz – lucky he didn't sell the birth certificate he found, but inevitable too since it is an enabling device to move the story on. They are on the run, and will remain so. 'Refuge itself was on the run'. They meet a Pole Boris knows: 'the first man we met who knew our real identity belonged to that section of the population which the invader had earmarked for degradation, for tasks that would never be more than those of underlings . . . but not for death'. The man's silence has clearly to be bought with money. Boris goes off to find a room. He and Naomi go for a walk. A German lieutenant invites them for a drink in the army mess. Boris looks out of the window. He senses something but engages in serious conversation with the soldier. He doesn't want to believe what he thinks he knows he saw, and nor do we: five men buried alive up to the neck. A soldier pisses on them. The *Shema*, the most important prayer in the Jewish liturgy, is slightly misquoted. The lieutenant hits Boris to discourage hysteria and in effect saves his life. The blow is a powerful device to shock us away from the horror, a clear sign that Rawicz is in control, and for the best reasons. The soldier attempts to reassure Boris by explaining that the buried men are Jews not Poles . . .

And now, in Chapter 20, there is an attempt to blackmail Boris. In an operatic, even melodramatic and farcical scene, Boris uses some of his own cyanide to kill the man. His mental toughness too is demonstrated, his iron nerve. Boris resolves yet again to gainsay comparison (is this a pre-emptive projection at avoidance of the inevitable genital showdown?), which would mean that what remains is that 'mere enumeration worthy only of a shopkeeper', in other words a work of memory rather than of understanding – the store being where we came in at the beginning of the novel. But the book, of course, is not an enumeration, not a documentary, any more than Lanzmann's *Shoah* is. It is an *oeuvre*, a finished work. Its constructedness (or artefactuality, if you prefer) is a self-ratifying justification of literary narrative, though not of the traditional kind, which cannot be trusted with such dangerous material.

Chapter 21. On the move, floating, unhoused, desperate, concealed in public like the Pelegs.[17] 'Uprootedness became our only homeland'. Now in Warsaw it would appear, he is beginning to chafe at the sexual fidelity to Naomi he is observing, but if he visited a whore she might give away the penile password. They have to move on for fear their identity is about to be revealed.

Chapter 22. Move move move; decisions; choice; more about putrefaction. Naomi has a long soliloquy. 'You didn't try to make love to me. I was disappointed. And I knew I wasn't going to be arrested or die before I had slept with you'. Compare and contrast the account in *The Last of the Just* of a desperate and magical lovemaking before death.

Chapter 23. Boris, according to his journal as presented by the narrator, has been reading the Upanishads and even written a poem[18] under their influence. He indulges in some philosophising, 'even though it in no way advances the main story'. A saloon bar *flâneur*, a Russian-style dreamer and talker,

Boris and the narrator – and one part of Rawicz himself – are the kind of figures you sometimes find floating around those who write books, like the acolytes around Joyce, acolytes Beckett fled from in horror. The narrator reveals a 'crucial dream' of Boris (see Chapter 31).

Chapter 24. Boris tells the story of his uncle.

Chapter 25. They must move on, yet again, Naomi having aroused suspicion. The relationship with Naomi is explored, yet again. They see slave labourers wearing the yellow star. She whispers in his ear: 'We are not yet the last'.[19]

Chapter 26–7. They reach a mountain resort. Boris understands that some people have a sixth sense towards those in disguise. He has to pretend to be anti-Jewish as well as non-Jewish. Sometimes 'I would derive a strange pleasure from reviling my people[20] and my family . . . The Law promulgated by God forbids members of my tribe[20] to touch dead bodies. Should I have conformed with that other Law which enjoins us from living in the company of murderers?' He has to outwit the major. Boris and Yuri 'quarrel' with each other. The situation is very dangerous and, once more, they move on. The net is closing in, their garb a rent garment.

PART THREE OF THE NOVEL

The Tool and the Thwarting of Comparisons

Prison, torture, Boris the brain, Boris the mouth, Boris the penis – or should we say Yuri? – for the story is almost entirely told in the third person, unlike the previous two sections,[21] *adding another twist to the narratological construction.*

In Chapter 28, the inevitable happens: Boris is arrested. He attempts to kill himself with cyanide, and is thwarted. His penis is revealed, the lettering there for all to read, like a stick of rock, an image from childhood as powerful as that of the gingerbread men. 'The tool and the art of comparison'.

In Chapter 29, Boris is seriously beaten up and transferred to another cell.

Chapter 30. The other people in the cell will die but Boris has a chance to live because he has admitted nothing. He shows his paces in a conversation with a cell mate. Yet again, the attempts to understand within his own parameters get him nowhere.

In Chapter 31, he is transferred to a cell where he is the only Jew. He has to clean the shit pail with his own hands. He is regularly interrogated; whipped. He keeps silent for two months. The 'crucial dream' of Chapter 23 actually 'happens' in this chapter, a radical example of narratological anti-linearity. Soon everything will change. Loneliness and despair are his lot, he cannot sink any lower into loneliness and despair.

Chapter 32. The impatient and exasperated interrogator, while sure Boris is a Jew, says at onc point: 'We've seen more than our fair share of "Poles" like you', which is not what Boris is claiming to be. This offers him an opening. He insists he is not a Pole, he is a Ukrainian. He demands that a fellow Ukrainian be sent to test him. The interrogator's professional pride as a Jew-detector is aroused.

Chapter 33. The game begins. Boris presents as an uncompromising Ukrainian nationalist to this Nazi collaborator sent to test him. The argument between them is strong, marvellous, fabulous: surely one of the great scenes in modern European literature, and one of the most powerful confrontations in a novel since the Grand Inquisitor scene in *The Brothers Karamazov.* The astonished interrogator looks on. The Ukrainian admits defeat: yes, Boris is a Ukrainian. All that remains is his signature, the circumcision, which Boris explains as resulting from an old infection and surgery to cure it. He quotes a doctor as saying that doctors can always tell the difference. Now he must be examined.

Chapter 34. The doctor cannot decide. Boris fancies the nurse. The case is referred up, to the military hospital.

Chapter 35. Boris is saved. The Major decides his circumcision was surgical, not religious. Back in the cell Boris/Yuri, now accepted as a kosher goy, is welcomed by the residents and told how sorry they are they treated him harshly but 'had you been in our shoes, would you have acted otherwise?' Boris, having got away with it (like the author himself in Auschwitz), muses that one day he will attempt to recapture the scene. The future is no more than a 'sign engraved on the skin of our minds'.

Coda. It is hinted in passing that Boris was deported to Auschwitz (Birch tree = Birkenau). But he survives, tool, comparisons and all. The coda returns us to the beginning: Full circle.

Post-script. 'This book is not a historical record'.

Notes to 'The Vocation of the Witness'

1 More about this in *I'm not even a Grownup*, my account of the diary of Jerzy Feliks Urman.

2 Leo L., 'for the sake of convenience let us call him L. L.', (Chapter 4) and Garin (Chapter 6), are partly based on two real figures from the L'wow ghetto, Leyb Landau and Salo Greiver – as the names suggest. According to the *Encyclopaedia of the Jewish Diaspora*, Landau, a famous lawyer, was head of the Galician branch of the Office of Jewish Self-Help at 12 Berenstein Street, whose main office was in Cracow, headed by the writer, Michael Weichert. The organisation was independent, not relying on local Jewish communities for support. Concerning Leo L., Rawicz has also used the fact that the third Chairman of the Jewish Council in the L'wow Ghetto, Dr Landsberg – who like his predecessors had a bottom line when it came to carrying out Nazi orders – was publicly hanged together with twelve Jewish policemen in late 1942, for refusing to carry out Nazi orders. See also Note 3 below.

In January 1942 a German businessman called Dr Dorman came to L'wow, hoping to establish tailoring workshops, using the cheap manpower available, namely Jews in the ghetto. He tried to negotiate with the German authorities – without success. But Salo Greiver, a Jewish merchant from Cracow, had established municipal workshops in Bochnia in western Galicia, hoping to save Jews from deportation. In L'wow, he probably worked in co-operation with Dorman. Greiver, an industrialist called Dr Deizler and a lawyer, David Schechter, managed the Jewish workshops in L'wow, which were established in April 1942 under the overall direction of Greiver.

3 It is extremely likely that Rawicz read the testimony of Rudolf Reder, who was one of only two survivors of Belzec. In this testimony, published in Cracow after the war and excerpted in Martin Gilbert's *Holocaust*, there is an account of the head of the Zamosc Judenrat being made to dance while the orchestra played.

4 The dates of this most famous of false Messiahs after Bar-Kochba are 1626–1676. Readers are referred to Scholem's article on him in the *Encyclopaedia Judaica*.

5 Jacob Frank (1726–1791) from Podolia was the founder of a Sabbatean Jewish sect, some of whose members (known as Doenmeh) could still be found in Turkey in the mid-20th century. They got up to a lot of mischief of a kind that might well have appealed to Rawicz – practical implementation of the antinomian heresy among the Frankists (although they wouldn't have called it that) included wife-swapping on Yom Kippur . . . To be fair to Piotr, he took Yom Kippur very seriously and always behaved correctly on the Sabbath of Sabbaths. More importantly, there was a link with L'wow, which Rawicz would have known about: 'In the stormy years between 1756 and 1760, a large part of Frank's followers converted to Catholicism, constituting a kind of Doenmeh in Poland, but in Catholic disguise. These events and especially the willingness of the Frankists to serve the interests of the Catholic clergy by publicly defending the blood libel in the disputation at L'wow (1759) deeply disturbed the Jewish communities of Poland'.

6 Aramaic phrase meaning 'the other side': a concept from the Cabbala referring to the dark or shadow side of the universe, hinting at a dualism not found in normative Judaism. See my letter in the magazine *Squiggle*.

7 One of the most popular of Jewish festivals, especially among children. The festival celebrates the defeat of the tyrant Haman, the major hate figure in Jewish history between Amalek and Hitler.

8 Janus Korczak was the founder and director of the Jewish Orphanage in Warsaw, which was run along the most progressive educational principles of the day. He was a pioneer of children's rights and was well known for incorporating the latest technologies in the classroom. Korczak was also a famous writer of children's books. He was transported with the orphanage children to Treblinka, where they were all murdered on 5 August 1942.

9 Naomi was the biblical mother of Ruth. Shulamith is the 'black and comely' maiden in the *Song of Songs*, and we also find her in Celan's 'Death Fugue'. In this great poem, the name, symbolising the Jewish people in exile, is counterpointed to the name of the classic German heroine, Goethe's Margareta. 'Your golden hair, Margareta / your ashen hair Shulamith'.

10 In orthodox circles, Cohens only attend funerals when they are primary mourners, that is spouse, sibling, parent or child, and they pray in a separate part of the hall. They are not allowed to touch a corpse. See Chapter 26 and Note 20.

11 See Note 1, *ibid.*

12 Mordecai Anielewicz was the overall commander of the combined Jewish fighting forces (with the exception of the right wing Revisionists who fought separately) in the Warsaw Ghetto. He was twenty-four when he died.

13 *op.cit.* Note 5 to Section 1

14 This chapter contains two of the ten brief extracts omitted in the English translation by Peter Wiles, now included in my revised translation (UK edition 2004). Peter Wiles does not remember excluding them, let alone the reasons why he or the author or the French or English-language publishers might have suggested it. See the Appendix for more details.

15 See also Note 2 above. The multifaceted question of complicity can at last be discussed in ways which were impossible until recently, often for understandable reasons. The archives are beginning to be published – as mentioned in the discussion on Chapter 6 and grey zones are being adumbrated. The head of the Jewish Council in Bialystock, Barash, was working with the Jewish resistance as well as for the Germans. Joshua Sobol has explored the personality of Gans in the Vilna ghetto in his fine play *Ghetto.* Primo Levi famously discusses the issue in *The Drowned and the*

Saved. Rawicz would have had no trouble agreeing with Bettelheim's comment from 1947: 'almost all those who survived the camps and could therefore report on their experience had in one way or another been beneficiaries of a class system whose lowest strata rarely survived'. See also George Oppen's poem 'Route' in *Of Being Numerous* (in *New Collected Poems).*

16 See Bibliography for details of her important memoir.

17 See Bibliography.

18

> For the sap of a poem
> And the rhythm of a plant
> Two different things,
> Brahmachari, they aren't.

I have slightly revised Wiles's translation, in order to get a b/b rhyme, as in the French.

19 In what seems to be the first article on Rawicz in France itself since the early interviews and reviews thirty four years ago, Anny Dayan Rosenman (see bibliography) reminds us about Kajik, the survivor interviewed in the film *Shoah*, who also feared he might be the last Jew on earth. One of the many conversations I miss having with Piotr is the one about Claude Lanzmann's *Shoah*, which came out three years after he died. The article by Dayan Rosenman appeared in the magazine which is edited by the director of *Shoah.* 'The phrase 'we are the last' occurs in various accounts of the last hanging in Auschwitz. The painter Zoran Music, as explained by Steven Jaron in his 2006 Adam Lecture at Kings College London, believed that 'we are not the last'.

20 As it happens, this quotation contained two rare mistakes by Wiles: 'peuple' should be translated not by 'race' but by 'people'; and 'tribu' is not a metaphorical word for 'religion' but a reference to the hereditary priests, the Cohens, and should therefore be translated by 'tribe'. Boris is a Cohen. See Chapter 8 and Note 10.

21 Anny Dayan Rosenman makes another good connection, reminding us that Appelfeld in *The Age of Wonders* tells the second section of his novel in the third person. Without casting any psychologistic aspersions on literary strategies, I would add that in the literature of the camps there are many relevant accounts of individuals splitting their selves as an instinctive or semi-conscious survival mechanism: Bettelheim, Heimler etc.

3

The Skin of My Soul

Note A

The virtually universal view of our friend is that he was a skirt chaser, *un coureur de jupes*, albeit an endearing one, who whether he left them or they left him remained good friends when the affair was over. There may have been an element of what I would call survivor's licence, mediated charm, but this was not the whole story. The link between this brilliant and wayward man's love affairs – one in particular – and his ongoing relationship with his wife not only when they lived together but also during the time of separation, and the connection between her death from cancer and his death, a few weeks later in her apartment, by his own hand (pulling the trigger of a pearl-handled shotgun, the best in Paris, bought while a bemused friend waited in the taxi), are painful and complicated and must await, if ever, another occasion or another writer. After his wife Anka died, he told one friend that 'God mixed in where he had no right to mix in', the God in whom he believed and whom he would worship on Yom Kippur – on one or two occasions with Elie Wiesel, Piotr told me – and at other times. Certainly Piotr felt remorse about Anka's death but the causes of suicide, like those of most great and fundamental turning points in life, are complex and over-determined, as I have tried to show in my work on Primo Levi.

The marriage of Anka and Pinkushek (Anka's affectionate Polish diminutive for Piotr's Hebrew name Pinchas) was a public psychodrama. The scene in the novel when Boris realises he must be faithful to Naomi for safety's sake (see Chapter 21, described in Section 2) does not reflect the real life scenario when Anka, exasperated by Piotr's sexual adventurism, threatened to report him to the Gestapo (the black humour perhaps being too much even for this novel). There were no children of the marriage (or of the love affairs), though his wife did have a miscarriage, around which time he did not cover himself with glory. They loved each other but she never completely trusted him.

Anka was a brilliant person in her own right, a film maker, hostess and woman deserving of her own memorial. Their mutual friends loved both of them. No one I spoke to knows when they got married (assuming they did) but Danilo Kiš, in his [auto]-biographical story about Rawicz, which is accurate in most respects, puts into Piotr's mouth the remark that the pair married in 1939 (though in the following sentence there is a blatant contradiction and another mistake, possibly in the translation rather than the original, namely that they got to know each other after the war and after emerging from the camps – Anka was not in a camp but in hiding; see also Note K below). However in this instance we cannot be certain that Kiš is accurate, partly because – according to a close family friend – Piotr and Anka met as students only in 1939, partly because another friend, though not so close, is certain they married after the war. The close family friend tells me that during the Soviet occupation Anka lived for some time in the home of Piotr's parents and that when they fled L'wow during the German occupation his – the friend's – parents, in order to help them, gave them some gold coins.

At the end of this note I append Czeslaw Milosz's poem about Anka. She signed herself 'Anka Rawicz' in her last testament written in hospital just before she died, which suggests that those correspondents who are of the opinion that Anka and Piotr never married are wrong. The account of her will in Danilo Kiš's story, published in French in 1993, is, I believe, substantially accurate.

Anka

CZESLAW MILOSZ

In what hat, from what epoch,
Is Anka posing in the photograph,
Above her brow the wing of a killed bird?
Now she is one of them, beyond the threshold
Where there are no men, no women,
And the prophet does not give separate sermons

To the ones covered with shawls
So that their long hair does not provoke lust,
And to the tanned, bearded men in draped burnouses.
Saved from the furnaces of World War Two,
Trying on dresses in reflected mirrors
And blouses and necklaces and rings,
With a hairstyle and makeup for the wars of her career,
Happy to go to bed or just talk over wine,
The owner of a beautiful apartment, full of sculpture.
Left to herself till the end of the world,
How does she manage now, fleshless?
And what could the prophet find to say, when he
has no thought
Of the hair under a shawl and the secret
Fragrance of skin and of ointments?

Translated by the author and *Robert Hass*

Note B

Suicide was, in the case of Piotr, an enduring preoccupation, but how much credence to give to a story Piotr told a friend of his – who told me – I know not: Piotr had attempted suicide at the age of five, when the old nanny in their apartment in L'wow told him his mother had not wanted to have him but could not get an abortion during the difficult period in the wake of the civil war which raged throughout her pregnancy (see Note C below). What is definitely the case is that there was much talk of suicide, and of the techniques available, among his friends, including Mrozek. 'At sixty, what do you die of? Cancer or suicide', said Piotr to a younger lover, accurately predicting the cause of his wife's death and announcing his own. Friends who suspected he was deadly serious could not talk him out of it. The end, on 21 May 1982, was terrible. Like Romain Gary, he shot himself in the mouth. The police would not allow anyone to see his body.

Piotr Rawicz

Lvov, Polyaka St. 3, Flat 11: the family apartment

Note C

Piotr's father Salomon, born in 1878, was a lawyer in L'wow, though not one of the most prosperous ones. He eventually became a member of the Bar Council of L'wow and was active in Jewish communal and charitable organisations. According to Sergei Kravtsov, a Soviet document prepared in 1945 concerning Jewish families murdered by the Nazis – to be presented as evidence at a war crimes court – was signed by Salomon Rawicz. L'wow was the capital of East Galicia, which had been the easternmost province of the Austro-Hungarian Empire and became part of Poland in the wake of World War One. Rawicz was born in L'wow on 12 July 1919 at the very end of the doomed nine-month long uprising which sought to establish the West Ukraine People's Republic. It was (and still is) an attractive and ethnically mixed city, 'Little Vienna' – the second city of Ukraine. I learned from a Warsaw genealogist, Michael Witwicki, that the ancestors of Rawicz certainly came from the small town of that name near Poznan. But there is no evidence linking Piotr's family to Alexander Rawicz (1800–1865) who co-founded the bank Hirschendorf and Rawicz.

In 1939 the Jews formed thirty-five per cent of the city's population, the third largest Jewish community in Poland. For details of their destiny, it is sufficient to read the entry on L'wow in the *Encyclopaedia Judaica* and Leon Wells's remarkable and critically important testimony, *The Janowska Road*, also known as *The Death Brigade*, and S. Szende's *The Promise Hitler Kept.* Rawicz often mentioned Wells to me and there is no doubt that the doomed Jewish world of Rawicz's home town (near Wells' small-town birthplace, but L'wow is where most of the action in *The Janowska Road* takes place) is the main geo-spiritual source of *Blood from the Sky.* Wells wrote to me as follows: 'Piotr was a very sensitive, very fine and very sad man. He was lost in this world, whose basic laws he did not understand'. The first sentence is true. I do not agree with the second one. Frank Stiffel, in his own vital book, *The Tale of the Ring: a Kaddish* and in correspondence is less taken with Rawicz's charms. Readers of Piotr Rawicz will also be interested in two very great older writers from the same background and region, Bruno Schulz from Drohobycz and Joseph Roth from Brody, who were exact contemporaries of each other.

Despite the early suicide attempt (see Note B above), Piotr was a cheerful boy, clever and destined for higher things. He was the youngest of three children (the older two, Marian and Stefa, left L'wow before the war) and attended a Polish gymnasium, obtaining his *matura* in 1937. He appears to have studied law for one semester in 1937–8 at the University of L'wow. He met his future wife at the university in 1939 but the next official record is of studies in 'Orientalism' (see student questionnaire translated below) at the University in 1940, under the Soviet occupation of East Galicia which followed the Nazi-Soviet Pact, and which lasted until the German invasion of the region after Germany declared war on the Soviet Union in 1941. Orientalism included literature, comparative religion and oriental languages. Like many scions of cultivated and relatively assimilated families in that region, Piotr did not have a *barmitzvah*. Rawicz was the exact contemporary of Paul Celan, born not far away in Czernowitz in the Bukovina, another province of former Austro-Hungary, but although Rawicz met Gisèle Celan-Lestrange in Paris he never met Paul, despite having close mutual friends. Piotr's family circle would have overlapped with people in L'wow who knew Bruno Schulz. Perhaps Piotr met relatives of mine from Stanislawow and Drohobycz, as he did further afield and unexpectedly, in Warsaw, where one of them, Ferdinand Vogel, actually changed his name to the less obviously Jewish one of Roman Rawicz, as a safety precaution. Piotr's family would holiday sometimes in the Carpathian mountains and elsewhere in the region, a land of compelling landscapes. Nowhere in the world is there a more beautiful and peaceful view of a river (the Dniester) than from the Karaite cemetery in Galich (Halicz), near the former Jewish cemetery, destroyed like the community itself.

Here is a translation of a form he completed – in imperfect Ukrainian – on 10 October 1940. I gloss only two points: first, he describes his father (and on another form himself) as a 'trudyashchi intelligent', a 'working-class professional', which was a sensible if transparent disguise under the Soviet occupation, though one should point out that by then his father was no longer a solicitor but was in employment as described in question 13. Second, unlike in western Europe, being Jewish was and is considered a matter of nationality, not religion.

QUESTIONNAIRE

(for students of the Ivan Franko L'vov State University)

Faculty: *Philology* Speciality: *Orientalism*

Course: *1 (2nd term)*

Will you study this course in the second term: *No*

1. Surname: *Rawicz*
   First name: *Petro* Patronymic: *Solomonovicz*
2. Sex: *Male*
3. Year of birth: *1919* Month: *July* Day: *12*
4. Region of birth: *Lvov Province: Lvov*
5. Nationality: *Jewish*
6. Party membership:
   a) Candidate member Communist Party
   b) Candidate member Communist Youth Union
7. Education: *Gymnasium. Matura in 1937.*
   (*One term Law department 1937–8*)
8. Social Origin: *Father is a working class professional*
9. Have you served in the army: *No*
10. Where your parents lived before September 17 1939: *Lvov*
11. Where they live now: *Lvov*
12. What your parents did before September 17, 1939:
    Father worked as a lawyer
13. What your parents do now:
    Father is director of a legal advice bureau
14. Home address of the student:
    Lvov, Polyaka St. 3, Flat 11

Date: *10/x 1940*

Signed: *Petro Solomonovic Rawicz*

Passport: *I-Zhp No 715677 Issued by 1st dept. S.R.M.NKVS, Lvov*

Date: *26/iv 1940 valid till 26/iv 1945*

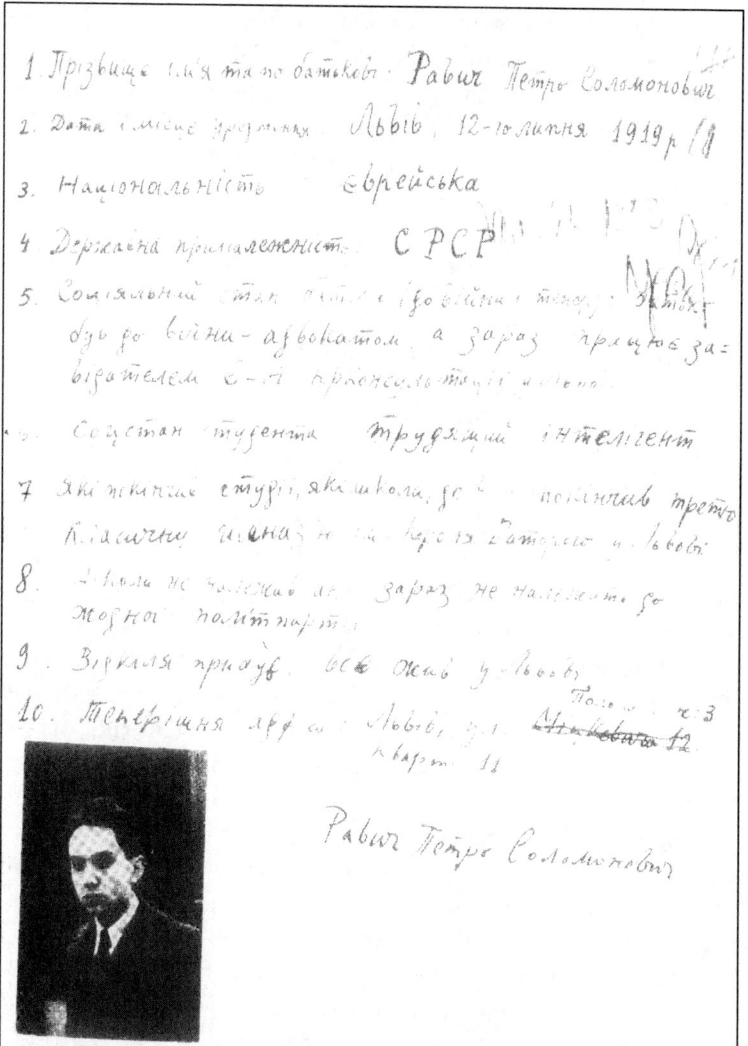

1. Прізвище, ім'я та по батькові: Равич Петро Соломонович

2. Дата і місце народження: Львів, 12-го липня 1919 р.

3. Національність: єврейська

4. Державна приналежність: СРСР

5. Соціяльний стан батьків (до війни і тепер): батько був до війни адвокатом, а зараз працює завідувачем [illegible]

6. Соцстан студента: трудящий інтелігент

7. Які скінчив студії, які школи, до [illegible]: покінчив третю класичну гімназію [illegible] Баторого в Львові

8. Ніколи не належав і зараз не належу до жодної політпартії

9. Звідкіля прибув: весь час жив у Львові

10. Теперішня адреса: Львів, ул. ~~[illegible]~~ [illegible] ч. 3 ~~12~~ кварт. 11

Равич Петро Соломонович

Student questionnaire dating from 1939 or early 1940

Above an earlier questionnaire is reproduced.

Among Rawicz's fellow students in the Oriental first year course, we find the following typically Jewish names: Szolom Cytron, Reuven Jerozolimski, Hanna Binkowska and Maria

Gruber. On another form Rawicz states that he graduated from the King Batory Third Classical Gymnasium in Lvov. Yet another form gives his mother's maiden name as Helena Sabina. Their address is given as Mickiewicz St, with an entrance on Polyaka St., known before 1938 as Brajerowska, and today as Galana Bichna Street.

Note D

Piotr arrived in Paris in 1947 already speaking excellent Ukrainian, Chochlis (Ukrainian dialect), Russian and German, in addition to his mother-tongue, Polish. Thus, the novel was written in his sixth language, French, which he mastered almost to the level of Beckett – this helps if you are going to produce a great French novel. Later, he added Sanskrit, Hindi, English, Yiddish and Hebrew and, for all I know, others – including possibly Spanish and Arabic. Even allowing for local multilingualism (Aharon Appelfeld, ex-Czernowitz, was unimpressed when I told him about Rawicz's languages), Rawicz was a seriously brilliant polyglot. Who knows if this did not inhibit him later? During the writing of the novel, his wife and various friends made suggestions for improvements in details (he sometimes complained about problems with French subjunctives), though opinions vary about the extent of his wife's contribution on a linguistic level. That she encouraged him in other ways is a fact, and that she encouraged him to be more productive is also a fact. By productive, we mean working up his multitudinous and graphomaniacal pieces of writing into a publishable form. No one is quite sure how long *Le Sang du ciel* took him to write. We may surmise that he paid a high price for the writing of such a work, but we would be cautious about naming it. The blurb of the original French edition states that this is the first novel 'he has written directly in French', suggesting that he abandoned earlier work, most likely written in Polish.

Piotr and Yiddish are referred to in a letter I received from André Schwarz-Bart (parts of which I translate here), in response to my correct suspicion that they knew each other and admired each other's great book.

My memory of Piotr is inseparable from my reading of his book, which has become a companion for me, a true companion for life . . . I remember his look which alighted upon everything with sweetness and irony; a look of extreme lightness, which never became heavy.

I remember a meeting in London with some old Yiddish writers. In Piotr's mouth this language, which I had associated with humble people, acquired an aristocratic cachet; and yet he expressed himself in a completely natural way. His pronunciation remains a mystery for me, a beautiful mystery.

That day Elie Wiesel improvised a short speech in honour of these old Yiddish writers who, for many reasons, seemed already to be not of our world, and we were all touched by the respectfully affectionate tone of the orator. But of all the visitors, the one who appeared most affected was Piotr Rawicz, who spent the rest of the day telling me how moved he had been and how impressed he was by Wiesel's ability to find the right tone and the appropriate words for these dear old writers. Six months later, he was still evoking the same tone and the exact words which Wiesel had deployed, to the point where I ended up thinking he had experienced the speech as being directed towards himself, as if he were an old Yiddish writer on the way out – in the guise of a brilliant and still young French novelist. Doubtless that was how he really saw himself, that at least is how it has seemed to me ever since.

Note E

Re-reading *Bloc-notes d'un contre-révolutionnaire* after a twenty year gap, I was struck by the fact that its tone was gentler and its attitude more generous than I had remembered. I suppose my own attitude at that time was more 'revolutionary' than it is now. It was not so much that Rawicz was countering revolution (except of course any hint of Stalinism), as countering a rival romanticism ('l'imagination au pouvoir' etc), and countering it with his own version. No question: even Rawicz, the laid-back *flâneur*, was challenged and aroused by the 'continuous carnival' – to use

Milosz's phrase from his review of the book – of the May Events; this high Romantic had found a worthy rival in the events, which generated the second and final book – a book which I am told annoyed P. Sollers enough to provoke him to punch Piotr during a live television discussion. Piotr wandered the streets throughout the month of carnival, read the events and his friends' reactions, and made comparisons (the explicit imaginative process central to *Blood from the Sky)*.

Much of *Bloc-notes* is a collage of the reflections of real and, I suspect, imaginary friends. X, for example, has to be a mouthpiece for Rawicz himself, coming up with what amounts to a perfect gloss on *Blood from the Sky:* 'No complaisance, no pity in the art of looking, every possible pity in the soul and in the intellect'. X again: 'When I was twenty I needed, like them [the students], extreme situations, a macabre landscape around me, death as close as possible . . . In one sense I was royally served by History between 1941 and 1945. Not long ago, Michel A. or another twenty year old showed me a manuscript. Revealing the same imperious need, I was ashamed of my ghetto, of my Auschwitz; like a millionaire faced with a beggar, I felt I was inside the skin of a vile capitalist, a vile shareholder [or rentier], in suffering'. *In propria persona*, Rawicz includes an epitaph between two paragraphs attributed to X, a perfect epitaph on Boris, if not on Rawicz himself: 'During all the periods of his life, his participation has been less active, his sufferings much greater, than the average. Have pity on the poor counterrevolutionaries'. In a dream narrative: 'I consider myself to be an expert in defeats, a specialist in humiliations undergone' – compare both Osip Mandelstam who made himself 'an expert in the science of goodbyes' and Piotr's friend the late Cioran who early considered himself 'a specialist in the problem of death', and let us not forget the specialities of Hamm and Clov in *Endgame*. Piotr and Cioran would spend whole nights walking through the streets of Paris, discussing ontology. This must have included Cioran's changing attitudes to the Jews, the subject of two important books reviewed by Joseph Frank, one about Cioran, the other about Cioran, Eliade and Ionesco. Maybe Piotr contributed to Cioran's development.

Rawicz received his French passport only in 1966, at which

point he was free at last to visit Poland: Auschwitz, Cracow, his aged father who thanks to his 'non Jewish looks' had survived the war, with a lady (perhaps a countess), in a *ménage à trois*, in relative comfort, on a Polish farm; free at last to stop smoking patriotic Gauloises and Gitanes; free at last to write the second book, which is quite political and which he, not yet being a proper Frenchman, might not have done if he had not possessed the precious document. Section 4 of this essay contains some longer extracts I have translated from *Bloc-notes*.

Note F

It was not altogether surprising to discover a similarity in these respects between Primo Levi and his close friend Jean Samuel (Pikolo), whom I visited in Strasbourg during my Rawicz research trip to France. Jean Samuel is a remarkable man, a classic survivor. It was obvious from the interview with him broadcast on BBC television in the late 1980s that he looks up to Levi. Samuel is inclined to be over-modest about his potential ability to tell his war in writing. I hope that one day he will elaborate on his privately circulated lecture to the Rotary Club of Colmar. It is interesting to compare the centrally important episode, when Primo Levi recites Dante to Jean Samuel in the famous chapter of *If This is a Man* ('The Canto of Ulysses'), with Jean Améry's expectation or hope in *At the Mind's Limits* that Hölderlin's famous poem 'Die Hälfte des Lebens', which the sight of a flag reminds him of, will awaken an emotional and mental response: 'But nothing happened. The poem no longer transcended reality. There it was and all that remained was objective statement: such and such, and the kapo roars 'left', and the soup was watery, and the flags are clanking in the wind. Perhaps the Hölderlin feeling, encased in psychic humus, would have surfaced if a comrade had been present whose mood would have been somewhat similar and to whom I could have recited the stanza. The worst was that one did not have this comrade; he was not in the work ranks, and where was he in the entire camp?'

One is also reminded of the critically important moment in Antelme's *L'Espèce humaine* when the French prisoners in

Gandersheim decide to have a meeting to express their solidarity with each other. Francis recites Du Bellay's most famous poem, including the lines 'Heureux qui comme Ulysse a fait un beau voyage . . . et puis est retourné, plein d'usage et raison' (strangely apposite to Levi's book *The Truce).* Francis has trouble saying the poem, 'anguished as if he had to express one of the rarest, most secret things ever given him to speak; as if he feared that, brutally, the poem might break in his mouth'. A fuller account of these episodes can be found in my essay 'Rescue Work: Memory and Text'.

Note G

After the war Rawicz intended to return to the university in L'wow to study history of religion and oriental languages but decided not to. He became a journalist, wrote poems, and wandered around Poland. In 1947 he received a scholarship to study oriental languages in Paris, and thus he resumed the formal education which had been so inconveniently interrupted by bad timing on the part of the Germans. Later, he took degrees in Hindi and Sanskrit, the latter at the Sorbonne, the former at what the blurb on the first English edition of his book bizarrely calls 'the Ecole Nationale for Living Oriental Languages'. (The blurb equally bizarrely states that his 'exploration of the possibilities of his chosen form will remind many of . . . Stravinsky'). In the early years in Paris, he worked as a diplomatic correspondent for foreign newspapers and for a while was press attaché to the Polish legation. Then there were several years of penury, although he did receive some reparations money. One of the jobs he had during the lean years was selling meat to Germany which met Germany's standards but not France's. A Mr Lübke was his opposite number. Later, when this gentleman had become President of West Germany, he was apparently overjoyed to see Rawicz among the journalists awaiting him as he emerged from the lift in the Hotel Bristol. Rawicz must have already begun work on his masterpiece. He received the 1962 Prix Rivarol after publication of the book in 1961 – a prize, now defunct, awarded each year for the best book written in French by a foreign national. There was a lot of drinking, a lot of sex (that he was a combination of Dostoevsky and Oblomov on the one hand and Auschwitz alumnus and sad clown on the other probably went down quite well), a lot of hanging out in the Coupole, the Flore and elsewhere – except when this self-confessed dilettante, this rootless cosmopolitan, this true believer, was writing. And he wrote every day, though much of the waking dreamer's writing, the sleepwalker's writing, was done at night. In the years when I knew him, there was no point in phoning rue du Lieuvin before 'lunchtime'. But then: 'Hello, my dear, how are you? I'll meet you for a drink in Sello's room, rue Galande, and then we'll have dinner in a little Russian restaurant where tourists don't go'. The drink would become two drinks, the dinner might not materialise, but no matter. The teacher's hand would be raised to his eye in a kind of limp salute, the head would go forward, and Piotr would launch into a free-flowing discourse about politics or Judaism or sexuality or Auschwitz or a fellow writer such as Wiesel or Kosinski, Rudnicki or Solzhenitsyn, Cioran or Schwartz-Bart, always beginning 'You see' or 'You see, my dear'. Not only in Paris. He visited London for medical reasons and we would always meet, but it is in Paris (or, in my imagination, in our mutual ancestral homeland of East Galicia) that I situate my affectionate memories of this extraordinary man, one of the most fascinating human beings I and others have been privileged to know.

After he received his prize, things began to look up: Jacqueline Piatier, the legendary literary editor of *Le Monde*, employed him as the freelance champion of and genuine expert on Slavic writers – such as Adolf Rudnicki (whom he also promoted and defended chez Gallimard), D. Kiš, Solzhenitsyn (who said of him that he was 'the first drunken Jew I have ever met' – Solzhenitsyn and I must move in different circles), Maximov, Sinyavsky, Witkiewicz, Gombrowicz, Mrozek etc. He served on literary juries, which financed trips to Germany, Israel and elsewhere, but he was never comfortably off. One friend insists that the Bohemian lifestyle – what I once called his 'ablative estate' (Emily Dickinson's phrase) – was in part at least a function of his poverty.

Note H

There are a lengthy unpublished journal written in several languages and other draft texts perhaps more obviously 'literary' filling two suitcases, which I hope to inspect at some point. Discussion with two people who have seen them lead me to believe that the journal is a huge rag bag of thoughts, reflections or reflexions, ideas, musings, reminders etc. etc. It is not impossible that an edited and abridged version of the journals could yield a simulacrum of an authentic Rawicz product such as he might have eventually composed himself (perhaps along the lines of Pessoa's posthumous *Book of Disquietude).* The same goes for the literary texts and for a severely pruned and edited collection of his occasional writings (prefaces, interventions in symposiums etc), his journalism (mainly on Slavic literature in *Le Monde* and elsewhere) and including – unedited – published stories, poetical texts and meditations on painters. These three books will only happen if someone makes them happen . . . . In Section 4 of this book, I include my translation of two of his poetical proses, of his unpublished essay on the painter Ernest Fuchs, of extracts from *Bloc-notes*. Here is a letter he wrote Claude Vigée.

Piotr Rawicz
13, rue du Lieuvin, Paris XV, France
Tel.: 531-37-53
Paris, 13 January 1968

Above, Dear Claude, is my new address. I have absolutely no excuse for taking so long to reply to your note and for not having told you how much I loved *Moisson de Canaan*[1] . . . I am knocking down an open door by repeating that you are a poet, a great and a true one, at a time when there are so many false and overrated reputations. Basically that's all I want to say to you about your book.

1 This book, published in 1967, contains Vigée's characteristic mix of verse and prose. Some of the poems in it are contained in *Flow Tide: Selected Poetry and Prose of Claude Vigée* – see Bibliography.

My long silence has been due, mainly, to the fact that I have had to move so many times, but this time, I think it's going to work: I have found a place which promises to be more or less stable although the notion of stability makes me smile, above all when it is applied to myself.[2] Madame [illegible][3] is about to send you a long letter. She doesn't seem to be very pleased with her film and hesitates, it seems, to show it to André Malraux or to his acolytes. But I shall be seeing it in the next few days and hope to form an opinion. In any case, she is very grateful for your good will and all your help. Likewise, dear Dolores speaks of you with emotion, and questions me from time to time on the subject of your next visit . . . As for me, I have just published a little poem in prose about Berlin, entitled 'La viande qui chante'[4] . . . in a small literary magazine; I am enjoying writing articles for *Le Monde* and try to work as little as possible. I am thinking of visiting Israel in the spring and rejoice in advance at the thought of the long alcoholic evenings we will, I hope, spend together.

Whether I shall come to Israel – to settle there or to die there – I have no idea. When it comes to resolve, unreliability and inconsistency have always marked my stay on earth, and I no longer dare believe in any of my resolutions. But however ridiculous it might appear, I would not want to die anywhere else than Israel. This is not a new tradition . . .[5]

Well, dear Claude, I was really happy to see you in Paris. That was a lovely gift of destiny.

2 And, indeed, he did not move flats again, though he killed himself in Anka's flat, where he lived for a few weeks after she died.

3 This word begins with a 'W' and could be Weyl, Wiesel, Weyel.

4 A translation of this text appears in Section 4.

5 Indeed it is not. The tradition of travelling to Israel to die (or, in the age of the jet, being taken there to be buried after dying in the Diaspora) goes back to the earliest years of post-Expulsion exile. Since the Redeemer, though he tarry, will make himself known, at the end of days, in the Holy Land, it is obviously more sensible for a resurrected body to be ready and waiting in the Land rather than have to make the long journey back from other countries. This is also, presumably, the reason why it is considered a good deed to bury some earth from *Erets Yisroel*, the land of Israel, in the coffin of a Jew who dies elsewhere.

I wish you and yours all the *very* best, and as this evening we are getting ready to toast the Russian New Year with Dolores, we will drink a bottle of vodka in honour of you, your happiness and your poetry.

Affectionately [signed Piotr]

PS [signed Dolores] I would like to write you a long letter, as if I already knew you well and for a long time.

Monsieur Claude Vigée,
27 Avenue Ben-Maimon, Jerusalem, Israel

Note J

Piotr's essays on Slavic writers such as Rudnicki yielded his most important published work apart from the novel, sections of *Bloc-notes* and the poetical texts. But in interviews and colloquia, he, like many writers (e.g Danilo Kiš), was not always at his best: even in *Bloc-notes*, we find such hyperbole as 'Behind every "collective fact", behind every grandiloquent social fact, I catch sight of, my system catches sight of, an anteroom of the gas-chamber'. Nor am I sure we learn very much from the following image found in his introduction to a colloquium session in 1974: 'for every writer, the language in which he writes is a kind of concentration camp. But when you write in a language not completely your own then it is a kind of prison within the camp, a second degree prison' (My friend Moris Farhi, who writes novels in his fifth language, English, strongly disagrees with me about this statement by Rawicz). But the continuation of the quote is a fine statement, which rings good and true: 'for me, French was always a bit like an inn, sometimes hospitable, sometimes unfriendly, sometimes uncomfortable. It was like a borrowed garment flapping about on my skin, on the skin of my soul. I am not saying it has been a completely negative phenomenon, for out of the perpetual battle with language sometimes certain values emerge, previously unpublished as it were. It is a sort of perpetual violation, a capricious mistress who allows variations on the erotic plane which are not considered classical but who will never be your legitimate wife, the Jewish mother who will never abandon you'.

In his introduction to the Cérisy colloquium on Solzhenitsyn – whom he had translated into Yiddish, championed persistently, and invited to Anka's salon in the flat on Boulevard Saint-Michel – he delivers himself of the following obiter dicta: 'I believe in God, in prayer, in the religious fact' and 'The only ethical obligation in a work of art is to fulfil itself completely, to be as adequate and faithful an incarnation as possible of its own kernel, its own germ, its own creative project. Do not give short weight. Do not judge an aircraft by the nature of its cargo'. Finally, and significantly, in the replies to Emil Fackenheim published at the end of Fackenheim's *Lecture to the Study Circle of Diaspora Jewry*, he says that 'the fate and condition of the Jewish people are the very essence of the human condition – the furthest borders of human destiny . . . And the fate of the 'Holocaust' Jew is the ontological essence of that ontological essence': this (and he makes the same point in his introduction to *Sablier* by Kiš) serves as another good gloss (see also in Note E above) on his hero Boris, though it is a view which in real life I no longer wholly agree with. This is the subject of another book. Would that Rawicz were around to discuss it with me: 'You see, my dear . . . ' For a start one would draw his attention to the discussion of Emile Fackenheim in M. A. Bernstein's important book.

Note K

Piotr's life was disrupted by the Nazi-Soviet Pact and the ensuing occupation of East Galicia, first by the Soviet Union in 1939 and then by the Germans in 1941. (Cousins in Sambor and Premszyl would also have been affected). Before he was arrested in Zakopane in Poland, near the Czech border in 1942, Piotr had spent a year with Anka wandering in that area. She managed to escape. In addition to some gold coins – see Note A above – they had false papers supplied by a friend. I understand that one reason for his fortitude under interrogation and torture was that he did not want to betray the names of those who had helped him. He even managed to explain away the *mezuzah* which for sentimental reasons he kept sewn in his jacket – he had, he said, bought the jacket on the black market and not noticed the small Jewish ritual object: Frank Stiffel tells part of Rawicz's story in his book. He meets Piotr in Cracow, and – a ghostly figure standing beside him in the urinals in the surgical block – in Auschwitz. In Auschwitz, too, Rawicz was close to the socialist Josef Cyrankiewicz, later Prime Minister of Poland for twenty years.

Having been deported to the camp in 1942 or 1943 as a Ukrainian, Rawicz successfully maintained the pretence of being the real thing, and not a Jew. He even had a medical certificate explaining away his circumcision, unlike Boris in the novel. Presumably Rawicz felt that the reader would think its existence was too good to be fictionally true. Despite all this, he was, unsurprisingly, suspected of being Jewish, and indeed a real Ukrainian was set against him to try to catch him out, just as in the novel; in the novel, however, the scene does not take place in the camp. Later he was suspected of being Jewish by two of the sidekicks of Bandera (the well known West Ukrainian fascist) and only quick thinking and fast talking saved him from being stabbed to death. But Rawicz was the first to admit that his experience of Auschwitz was not the worst possible – he even received letters and parcels from Anka, whose life in Cracow throughout the war was extremely unpleasant and dangerous: some of the time she worked as a maid for Germans while pretending to be a Ukrainian from Kiev (like Piotr/Boris she too could pass) and often had to flee – once jumping out of a window – when someone suspected something.

By now you will not be surprised that our friend's sexual ardour was not diminished in the camp, but the experience of servitude scarred him and surely consolidated a fundamental aspect of his world view – his combination of low cynicism and high romanticism. Perhaps this combination contributed to his survival. He told me that he had had an SS officer's wife as a mistress in Auschwitz which, if true, was a much more risky activity than the masturbation which was the only heterosexual or perhaps I should say non homosexual alternative on offer for the minority whose libidos were still functional. He wrote love letters for the less bright kapos ('la connerie est une maladie incurable' – which can be translated as 'being a dickhead is an incurable illness') in exchange for sausages. Once – he told me –

tottering back to his block after a drinking session (punishable by death), he saw a man and a boy making love near the latrines. 'Love is the greatest thing in the world', he thought to himself. Their misdemeanour was discovered and Piotr was able to save them from death only by pleading with a superior to accept a bribe, money stolen from a corpse. But there was a condition attached to the acceptance of the bribe, the playing out of a mean trick. Told they were to be castrated, the two men were duly led off to the surgical block. The younger one was pissing himself with fear, the older one crying and saying he had not made love to a woman in all his twenty six years. They were injected. When they awoke, with huge bandages, they thought the worst had happened . . . which it hadn't. They thanked Piotr. Piotr Rawicz left Auschwitz for Leitmeritz, a camp near Theresienstadt in former Czechoslovakia, in 1944, where he stayed until the inmates were liberated in 1945.

4

The Holy Germination

The Companion of a Dream

The dream has the hardness of stone; an arid dream, burning stones. Humidity would be compassion. It is absent like compassion.

The nightmare town, still invisible, is on the move. Very close, hidden by the dust's red curtain, it will fall with a crash on empty huts. Very soon or in a thousand years, its evil creeping stems, its feelers will throw themselves over this leprous desert and throttle the whole zone.

A false Moses arises in the zone. Moses-scorpion among the men-scorpions. This Moses is dumb, his hearers deaf. They had all climbed this mountain which is only a heap of dustbins welded together by dry clay. They were frozen still, during their climb. Immobility is only a frozen swarming. Silence is but an imprisoned howl, choked before crossing the threshold of sonority.

Clumsy actors play before blind spectators. The rays of light find few eyes to wound, nothing but empty sockets.

And yet, all mutilation is holy, so holy it passes the contagion of its holiness on to the One who mutilates. From the wedding between the holy Mutilator and the holy Mutilated are born children in shapes hitherto unknown, issuing from an ancient bestiary.

Space is a piece of clothing worn inside out by a hump-backed clown. No more clown – and the clothing floats in search of a shape, a flesh to clothe. Space is a stinging bumble-bee whose sting was torn out. A heel crushed the buzzing insect; its broken carapace dried up and is only a dead scale. Space is dead. Space is no more.

Formerly, in another life, the bumble-bees subsisted on living honey and on dead honey. We are the dead honey. And even the death of honey.

Between you and me, Lord, you have established that isolating stratum named Reality. You have made me its co-creator, have imposed on me that repugnant work. And it eats away at both of us, becomes encrusted in our flesh like an insatiable rust.

Moses broke the Tables of the Law and, not receiving any others, leaves with a tiny bundle, lost in the crowd. He is nothing but an anonymous mound, a tiny cell of the heaving Beast, recently arisen and yet eternal, named *Galut*, Diaspora. And since space is dead, since Distances have disappeared, like bits of string burnt in the fire, Sand turns into Snow.

Become man with a bull's head, the Scorpion crossed rivers, plains, forests. In a lost village of Siberia, during the long evenings, little peasant girls whisper eulogies of a benign Minotaur who procures efficacious herbs for them, tells their fortune.

The frost sparkles beyond the red. The *Aurora Borealis* pours its cold fire on the snow. A hunt is about to begin. Am I the hunted? Am I hunter? And if the reindeers, my brothers, manage to escape, how shall I look at the sad eyes of the hunters, returning disappointed with empty hands?

Well, I shall be the arrow, but at the same time I shall be the target towards which it flies, and the hunter who releases it from his bow. And I shall be the arrow's flight.

But before the spectacle begins, I shall secretly relive the stages of this voyage which has led from the sand desert to the snow desert.

Somewhere in Morocco, on the edge of an oasis swallowed by a dream, I have laid siege to an old castle, I have become castle. Pilgrims, proud horsemen, filthy beggars rested in my shade. Impassive, I fixed my blind battlements on them, my empty loopholes.

Each of them repaid my hospitality by leaving me a small piece of their earthly fate. The old walls have become motley, like the destiny of humans. Tired of this multitude of colours, one day the castle flew away on its powerful wings to be merged with a passing rainbow in the distant sky.

Harlequin in Verona, I showed off my small tricks to an audience of children. They threw their smiles and sweets in my direction. Clothed in rags, a blonde girl whose velvet look weighed like lead whispered her fear and her loves in my ear.

Old crones took a child's corpse away. Before the jubilant eyes of the teeming, rejoicing crowd, the Town's solemn servants mount the witch on the stake, tie her with cords, transmit the kiss of torches to the dry wood. Like a flock of sparrows, the white nudity flies away, scatters in the crowd. Each sparrow turns into a silver blade, sharpened, and the blade plunges into the eyes of the men in the front row, avidly watching the spectacle.

When the flames had accomplished their task, people noticed that the witch was a small white goat.

As a gardener in a Granada suburb, I cultivated a plant, a single one. Faithful to my scorpion's past I dedicated my work to a cactus. I had cause to regret it. Thorns began to grow inside. Heavy drops fell from a flayed heart. Was it mine? Is not every heart in this valley mine? – open your eyes and, at the frontiers of the sea, look at these raspberry-coloured pebbles that live and fly away.

Henceforth, the thorny plant was nothing but a breathless machine. Once more, I took up my pilgrim's staff. Then it was roads again, naked and indecent like a shameful baldness. A tree, a single tree, would be compassion. The tree is absent, like compassion. Nothing but blind signposts, without directions, pointing nowhere and jeering at our final weariness.

The horizon, contracted like a funnel, is filled with small dull houses, that have no chimneys, no opening. Their doors and windows are fastened.

These roads are an eczema. The last chariot passed by an eternity ago, leaving behind Definitive Ruts; the roads – metallic stems imprisoning my skull. I tore myself away and I ran, ran endlessly. It was there that the head took on the shape of a bull.

Nothing has remained in me but belief that is too great.

Woven with all the fibres of my body and spirit, this faith does not retreat before any blasphemy, before any prayer. But when faith overflows, is lost in its own ecstasy, could there be any flame untainted by blasphemy?

Lying immersed in the red dust, I listened, within myself, to these words: 'According to the Scriptures, You created man. What a joke!'

Or, at least, what a simplification! What you have really created is suffering – the one solidly built frame. It was only afterwards that you laid out on this black, oak stage, on this universal framework – a rag named 'man'. This tattered garment is only cut up as a function of, to the measurement of, its unchanging framework: grief.

Was it on my lips or in my heart these impious words arose?

The rest of the journey was made in the hollow of a Giant Hand that raised up the vagabond. Out of the whistling of two winds breathless from a last combat, out of the rattle of two tempests biting and devouring each other, escapes the chanting of a psalm, a lamentation in dialogue: 'Poetry is yellow fever, the malady of language! – No, the malady of silence . . . '

Poetry is the conflagration of language!

No, the conflagration of silence, ultimate silence.

We went on by. In farthest Siberia, a thousand mirrors dance beneath a snow hill. Out of the last mirror I took a sickly foetus with almond eyes. Was it my hot breath or my humid nostrils or even my compassion? Poor I am, with only have my breath to give. A great love is born which buys back pasts and futures. Which vibrates like the Ultimate Silence.

Singing Meat (Berlin Pages)

Gold flecks in the eyes of frogs or even lizards – let the zoologists answer that question –, the sleepy surface of the pond covered with thick white leaves, the rebuilt castle, indecent in its white nudity, filled with ridiculous floating 'mementos' that belong to nobody; grinning belfries – real or false (twilight is a sly and crafty sculptor), the long shady lanes, each a dumb song, and the little girl, the very fair one, climbing a tree, coming down, bending over and straightening up with a gymnast's movements – *eins zwei, eins zwei* – the contours of her body, those curves, those animated curls, those swellings and spheres wound your guts, give rise to a lewd prayer; the afternoon is dying, the very dense hour made of glazed drops of dew settles on the motionless park. At present, this city is a water-lily, the 'maxim' of a water-lily, a moment of reverie of a water-lily. It is time for you to leave the city.

Your ignorance of the City was dear to you, and you trembled over it like a mother by the cradle of a sick child. For this ignorance was going to blanch, you were fully aware of that; it was going to die and give place to a knowledge; incomplete, biased, false, rickety, pretentious as any human knowledge. As a lover of flights, not at all blasé about them, (has a dictionary of flights ever been considered?!), you must flee the city before the ugliest period begins: that of well-rounded formulas, of generalisations. Bring along your love of swamps and twilights, your love of abundant blond bodies, contaminated (as is stupidly said) and very clean. They open and submit. They vibrate slowly. They only awaken to confront their own sweet astonishment and they do not know the History lurking in their folds and pigments. Are you now their only attentive reader, their only legitimate master?

Tomorrow or in one year, your plane will find its way among the multicoloured clouds that it will seek to violate and that are inviolable. Somewhere, around Sunset, your humble grooves await you. She will be there, likewise, awaiting you, the one who never waits for you, who exasperates you for she flees you and does not leave you; but you know she is crazy about the display you lack and the insecurity you abound in. To caress the pale gold that will gently vibrate beneath your hands, you will have to pretend you are a living man. This exercise is not absolutely safe when you get out of practice.

Here, in this city, even if you asserted the opposite, no getting away from it: you enjoy the sovereignty of a statue, of a master dead six million times. Is it your fault if you can only assume this thankless role by playing the clown? You have to be a Jew and born among the Scythians, you have to be a coloured man into the bargain, for the doors, the hearts, and the rest of it, to open in the city of Berlin . . . According to the colour of your skin almost, you 'fulfil the conditions'. For the first time. No resistance on the part of matter, objects, men and women. When your sound-proof, phantasmal lift broke down for two minutes, you were relieved. At what hour, then, will the dream change into nightmare?

But first of all, is B . . . really a city, with its teutonic guts, its American epidermis, its pure country air and its scattered passers-by? Or is it a series of lakes issued from an ancient tale, set in dark forests, dotted, at the pleasure of a caprice, with small inhabited islands? These proud, anaemic buildings, studious and unconcerned, rise without faith in full flight – which is already the beginning of absence . . . Will they be swept away like a movie set on the very day when, weary of sleeping between the lines of a poem, the 'Scythian' prophecy of Alexander Blok begins to take on flesh?

Questions! Questions! They are like the churches of the city, too new: the carillons that chime like all the bells in the world, but whose sound seems a 'synthetic' nothing . . . Am I in a hurry or am I afraid to rediscover this moribund desire, this defeat incarnate over there, in Paris? My false medieval madonna with her consumptive beauty, her golden tortoise smile, with her genius for void that forces me to exist a little, for someone has to pay the rent. Must you then hurry to such an extent to confront this army of collusive dreams which attach you, one to the other, like a hidden crime, and that you happen to fight with the secret hope they will be your conquerors?

That night, my dear, there were five dog-headed men, no, wait, five man-headed dogs, acting scientifically on stage. They revealed the rules to me. They were obeying the finger and the eye of a man whose skin was green. At night, this man sometimes transformed himself into a stately castle. He threw the dogs some small almost extinguished suns as food; wailing could be heard . . .

Then I cohabited with a fish which rubbed my back. His touch was gentle, like yours. He learned the tirades of Shakespeare by heart. He sweated. What is the sweat of fish like? Don't be jealous. My fish was a bit like you. He rubbed my back and I was the rubbing, or the rubbing was you. Isn't it the same thing? Later, I was water-lily . . . But no, wait, it would have been too heavy . . . I was just the fugitive maxim, a moment of reverie of a water-lily . . .

I feel that this city, likewise, is a water-lily. My departure plane will violate a giant rainbow whose two water-lilies will be the pylons. The blood of a water-lily? Of a rainbow?

Those dreams whose musical offering over there, in the West, she brings me at every awakening, those dreams that I shall have to return to, are made of coloured glass like awkward fairground angels, hanging from a Christmas tree in a peasant's hut. I break them without pity. I throw them against the massive paving-stones of Paris. And they extricate themselves from their original form as they give forth their brief 'last sound', plaintive and sweet, like the beginning of a lullaby. And you swallow the crushed glass but you know: 'This has no effect, this does not carry any consequences . . . '

A quarter of a century ago, in a death cell where the emissaries of this city shut you up, you swallowed a quantity of it.[1] And you survived. That, at least, is what is claimed. And then, other dreams are reborn in a garret in an old quarter of Paris between a man and a woman who do not succeed in loving each other, for they are but a single non-being.

Extracts from *Bloc-notes d'un contre-révolutionnaire*

I was in the small Ukrainian town B. where my father was born. I was with one of my Parisian friends; he was lost in the Chagallian landscape. Twilight gave way to night. Feeling myself responsible for my companion's well-being, I left him somewhere, in a little old inn, and I was annoyed with myself; but at the same time I wanted nothing to do with this companion, this witness to my false life, my urban Western life. The old wooden synagogue, which I knew had been burned down, was there, and the great lake, asleep, studded with nocturnal water-lilies that gave forth brief plaintive sounds, that lake situated higher than the town sheltering behind a dam. The dam was built by Tartar prisoners in the sixteenth century . . . impenetrable forests all around. Oh how I belonged to this ancestral landscape, at this moment of very ancient, very Jewish history! The lost child, the prodigal son returning from the 'great world', rediscovering his cradle and the cradle of his cradle, his seed and the seed of his seed . . . I recalled the G. family, relatives of ours. I knew that Hitler[2] had exterminated them, but I sought and found their house, and found them in that huge house. I was shown through a stable, a cow-shed, a hay-barn, through manifold dark corridors into the boudoir of my aunt Miriam who,

1 In Chapter 28 of the novel (see Section 2 of this book) Boris is prevented by his captors from swallowing a phial of cyanide.

2 My friend F. L., rereading these words, observes that Hitler is only one of the innumerable names with which we rig out . . . Time. (Author's comment)

at forty, regal and opulent, sent voluptuous thrills through me when I was fifteen. She kissed me, happy but not in the least surprised by my presence. All of a sudden, some devilish little dogs appeared, moving about rapidly on two paws, grotesque, chattering, yelping, ironical, wearing maids' pinafores and red cloaks embroidered with white. Their skills, their cloaks . . . Did this reveal the exaggerated attentions of a slightly cranky mistress of a house in a small town? Or was it Hell, the Devil's power? The febrile excitement and evil irony of these impudent dogs made me feel I was really 'on the other side',[3] behind Being, beneath the very lining of Being. We were in Russia, and that reassured me, in my Jewish Russia of the old days. It was a more successful return than I would ever have believed, but even so it was incomplete, fragmentary, riddled with holes. The sky breathed slowly, painfully, a sick sky. Candles burned themselves out in branched candlesticks. Copper and dark wood becoming light. Why did I leave this world, the only one I had?

So many recesses, so much meandering among the heavy pieces of furniture in this low room. In one corner I noticed a large piece or roll of fabric. I think it was black velvet, sparkling and iridescent. A suspicion touched me: was my aunt Miriam engaging in speculation, dealing on the black market? This thought was unwelcome to my vanity. Whatever does death, does this regime, reduce decent people to? All of a sudden, the huge piece of velvet began to move slowly, then quicker and quicker. I noticed that it was in fact the powerful wing of a bird. But what bird? Endowed with intelligence, the wing sought its invisible, perhaps non-existent bearer. Was it a hydra or a huge prehistoric bird that the nostalgia felt by this orphaned wing prepared itself to call forth from Nothingness with magical movements? (A quick thought, barely formulated: I must revive a science symmetrical to ontology: nontology).[4] Suddenly a black sheep appeared, began to grow and shrink in an irregular rhythm; now threatening to fill the whole room with its

3 Perhaps a reference to *sitra akhra* (See Note 6, Section 2)

4 The invented word 'nontology' is my attempt at a translation of Rawicz's invented word 'néantologie'. There is no suitable equivalent semantic antonym in English – 'nothingnessology' won't do – so a

presence, now confining itself to the dimensions of a toy. The wing which, meanwhile, had become several wings, 'adopted' the sheep which flew towards the black ventilator, breaking window-panes, flying towards the moon with an infernal noise. The greenish moon, larger than life, exploded in an uproar like a shell. The ringing of the telephone woke me up.

At that moment, still half asleep and no longer finding the impudent little dogs beside me, I thought I heard these apparently incoherent words coming from within me: I often think of God and of my death. I often think about 'the other side'. Hell, doubtless, exists on the other side. And there is a strong risk I shall find myself there. Well, too bad. The sooner the better. My excessive, always insatiate, love . . . for the past.

* * *

My prayers shrink, they become mean and rotten. Yet, how can one live without prayer? . . . Mean, tight, rotten . . . but prayer.

Prayer is the living sky one can touch throughout one's entire life, a gate through which one can enter a whole string of palaces that breathe, that no longer belong to our world down below.

And if your God was only blind infatuation . . . So what!

* * *

A teacher set the pupils in his class a very difficult mathematical problem, a complicated equation. The clever ones, the top ones that year, struggle to find a solution by the sweat of their brow . . . without success. For the problem is insoluble, there is an error in the statement of the problem. But with the master's authority backing up this statement, no one dares imagine there could be a mistake at the core.

According to S.N., God is the teacher in question. The mathematical problem is life, and we are the pupils.

* * *

morphological antonym (despite the mixing of Latin and Greek) was the only option. 1972. (1995. I still can't improve on 'nontology'); (2006. No change)

Feeling alone, I devise the theory of a whole string of countless 'me's serving as my companions. As if I were presented with photos of myself taken every year, every week, every day, every second, every millionth of a second, from birth or better still from conception. Only it is not a question of photos but of models of these hypothetical photos. And the photos or rather the models are not drawn only from my past but equally, if the word has any meaning, from my 'future'. (I notice that I am unable to write the word 'future' without inverted commas). Till the day I die, and even later, till my skin and bones rot, till their rendezvous with destiny in the entrails of the worms that will have eaten them. And later still.

And so I find myself in this huge infinite procession of my doubles, no! of my past 'me's', and those to come. They are fraternal companions. I love neither my present 'I' nor my former 'I's nor those to come. We cross the desert together. But this desert is not bordered by a Promised Land.

Which of them behave most strangely, even hostilely towards me? The diluted down-at-heel 'I's of the past? Or those to come?

To grow old, I have been assured, is to feel less. Old age is the state of a body (and a soul) that is disintegrating and would like to be treated as if it were not . . .

Moreover: between the 'I' [je] and the game [jeu] looms one little letter, completely insignificant. But this little letter changes everything, arranges everything in favour of the 'game' as opposed to the 'I'.

What game is it? Who is the croupier, the hidden controller? . . .

Doubtless a cosmic kapo, an assistant god, somewhere, must be laughing, laughing . . .

Never write the words 'I' and 'me' . . . except between inverted commas.

The Tohu-Bohu, the Demiurge and the Holy Germination

'The man goes out into the night. His groping foot breaks the surface of the thick waters. He plunges into the tranquil pond strewn with aquatic plants. His fingers touch the distant and black sky, the sky which is breathing heavily. Like touchy islets, like carnal and rubescent flames, the thousands of breasts of all the women he has loved, of all those he ought to have loved, living stalactites, decorate the sky which rises and falls in a breathing ever more rapid. That the man plunges into the pond in order that he might himself become pond once more, what does it matter! Meanwhile his thousand mouths pump white milk and black milk from a thousand orifices. His snooping and avid tongue licks the sour juice from a thousand slits which stand out against the sky lit up all of a sudden, like a thousand sparks, a thousand flashes. The mother of all suffering: that of shadows changing into light . . . '

'Love . . . it's for butchers: you have to know how to handle the meat with cruelty and dexterity. Coldly. Calculate losses and profits. Curses on the butcher who for a fraction of a second has experienced the temptation to become the meat on his own stall!'

'Is orgasm the only ambassador, the only true messenger of the Divine in this poor world?'

> 'Islet of discordant vibrations
> dumps of grindings frozen on the threshold of sonority
> maze of suppressed howls, of bastard howls
> man, man lost in the immensity of the plain
> tireless dupe of winks given you by your gods,
> infinity
> love
> your neighbours
> lakes, mountains and dead waters
> woman
> and the whole gang of hired servants of the absolute,
> I who am but the plaything of my own inept reveries,
> you are my brother, how could I push you away?'

Like venomous black serpents, whistling, spitting, these blasphemies and so many others assail you when confronted by the pictures of Fuchs, the monsters of Fuchs. For in them, salvation is coiled up – and your impatience becomes feverish.

The old legend:

Before time began, matter lay there inert. In its bosom – concave events deader than death. Primal vibration, holy and shameless germination, blinding abundance – whence do they come?

Is it that bearded demiurge, laden with a thousand multi-coloured headgears? That patriarch of the people of the unicorns? That cruel Assyrian king, welcoming and joyful, who tirelessly conducts his loving battle against the Torah, for the Torah?

The most ancient, the most hidden myths feed from his hand like a white goat and a black goat. They become flesh, and flesh, before our eyes, changes into myth in a sonorous coming and going – the panting of the cosmos. And desire engenders flesh, flesh – desire which climbs, which marries the curves of the biblical tales engraved somewhere, behind the lining of being. Is it clinging to the skin of our souls?

The seven days of creation are perpetuated endlessly. Angels climb and descend Jacob's ladder.

(Have you ever tasted angel flesh, allowed its sap to stain your vestal robes?!)

In the beginning was the word. But wasn't desire, then, lurking in its inner walls, before the beginning?

'Thanks to prayer, prayer without respite, its entrails have become its epidermis; its epidermis its entrails, the one and the other devoured by nostalgia for their previous state. At the crossing point of these two nostalgias rise green sparks which are dying, which are dying'.

Shame on the pathetic three dimensions with their ridiculous pretensions, pretensions to reign over palpable reality. Let them be restored to their proper place, which is modest. Distances are abolished, dams are broken: between the past and the present, the already and the again, between the animate and what is wrongly called the inanimate.

Carnal fireworks ('your fingers have pulped, torn, pierced the kin of the flame; you have penetrated the flesh of the flame') light up the festival, the little game of totality, the only one which matters. I would be betraying you and betraying myself if I were to reject the last word which remains to be uttered: genius.

5

Commented Bibliography: Piotr Rawicz

Books by Piotr Rawicz

Le Sang du ciel, Gallimard, 1961 reprinted 1982.

Translation by Peter Wiles, as *Blood from the Sky,* Secker and Warburg/ Harcourt Brace, 1964. Reissued, with a new introduction by Lawrence Langer, Yale University Press, 2003. Republished in a revised translation and with a new Preface and Afterword by Anthony Rudolf, Elliott and Thompson, London 2004. The Afterword is reprinted on the website of Ready Steady Book. The novel has also been translated into Italian and Polish, the latter edition with an introduction by Hélène Cixous.

Bloc-notes d'un contre-révolutionnaire (ou la gueule de bois), Gallimard, 1969

Texts by Piotr Rawicz in other books

From Bergen Belsen to Jerusalem: Contemporary Impressions of the Holocaust by E. Fackenheim, World Jewish Congress, Jerusalem, 1971

One of the Replies is by PR.

Solzhenitsyn: Colloque de Cérisy by R. Tarr (ed.), Editions 1018, 1974

Text by PR entitled 'Ethique et esthétique: le rapport à l'occident'. See also his interventions in discussions.

Paintings by Ernest Fuchs, Galérie Verrière, 1974

Text by PR entitled 'Le Tohu-bohu, le demiurge et la sainte germination', included in the present volume.

Solitude d'Israel, J. Halpérin and G. Levitte (eds), PUF for World Jewish Congress, 1975

Text by PR entitled 'Solitude juive et création littéraire'. See also his interventions in discussions.

Le Lion de Saint Sabbath by Adolf Rudnicki, Gallimard, 1979

Introduction by PR.

Politique et religion, J. Halpérin and G. Levitte (eds), Gallimard, 1981

Text by PR entitled 'Reply to Manès Sperber'.

Sablier by Danilo Kiš, Gallimard, 1982

Introduction by PR.

Selected contributions by Piotr Rawicz to periodicals and journals

Interview with PR (Nicole Dethoor), *Combat*, 5 October, 1961

Interview with PR (Anna Langfus), *L'Arche*, February 1962

Review of *August* 1914 by A. Solzhenitsyn (first Russian language edition), *Le Monde*, 2 July 1971

Review of *Oeuvres complètes* by S. I. Witkiewicz, *Le Nouvel Observateur*, no 867, 22–28 June 1981

In a footnote, the editors – rightly unwilling to censor our friend – dissociate themselves from a daft and extreme political point made by him. How well I remember that kind of argument when he was feeling bolshie, or, rather, anti-bolshie. However, in his introduction to a Rudnicki story (for other details see under *European Judaism* below), he implicitly defends the more conciliatory approach of the author.

Contributions by Piotr Rawicz to *European Judaism*

PR was on the editorial board of this London/Amsterdam bi-annual magazine, with which I was associated as literary editor and then as editor from 1970 till 1975. He recommended other writers to the journal, and himself contributed to the following issues.

No 9, 1970. 'The Companion of the Dream', translation by Anthony Rudolf, included in the present volume

No 11, 1971. 'Singing Meat (Berlin Pages)', translation by Anthony Rudolf, included in the present volume

This issue also contains the edited transcript of the magazine's Paris Colloquium in which Rawicz participated, along with A. Alvarez, Lionel Blue, Albert Friedlander, Michael Goulston and myself from the magazine, and from France, among others, Hélène Cixous, E. Levinas and Albert Memmi. Paul Auster, then living in Paris, and I acted as unofficial translators. Unfortunately Auster has only the vaguest recollection of Piotr.

No 13, 1972. 'Fragments' (from *Bloc-notes*), translation by Anthony Rudolf, included in the present volume

No 14, 1973. Introduction to a story by Adolf Rudnicki, translation by Susan Knight

This text revises an article Rawicz wrote for *Le Monde* in 1966. Among many interesting points we find: 'As opposed to an Elie Wiesel or an André Schwarz-Bart, whose vocations as writers have somehow been inspired and conditioned by the Nazi genocide, Adolf Rudnicki endured the Apocalypse as a writer, still young but already in full possession of his powers'.

No 23, 1978. 'Salt and Pepper', translator unknown

'I do not know if we the walking wounded know everything or nothing best. I only know that all my wanderings, from high places to the lower depths, all those words spoken and unspoken, the camp and Paris, Ukraine and France, Auschwitz and Jerusalem . . . they are all a part of me, they are me and will stay with me to my dying breath, I nearly forgot: there is also that army of dreams that descends nightly and becomes flesh to devour the thin flesh of my incredulity.'

Fiction about Piotr Rawicz

Jurgenson, Luba, *Le Soldat de papier*, Albin Michel, 1989

There is an intended touch of Piotr in the character of the poet in this novel.

Kiš, Danilo, 'Youri Goletz' in *La Règle du jeu*, 9, 1993

This troubling story, according to a prefatory note, was composed in 1983–4, after Piotr's death in 1982 and around the time of the stories collected in *The Encyclopaedia of the Dead*, but the author unsurprisingly preferred to keep it separate – it is far more autobiographical than the other stories. This French version was its first publication in any language. The eponymous hero is named after Boris's alter ego, and is based on Rawicz himself, who was a friend of Kiš and wrote about his work in a preface to Sablier (see Bibliography above). According to Kiš's post-scriptum, the fictionalised Rawicz 'remains half way between reality and the world of platonic concepts'. Most of the factual material about Piotr is historically accurate, Piotr's mood in the last months of his life is well captured, and something of his wife's personality (ef Milosz's poem in Section 3 of this book) and their marriage comes through. The account of his search for a gun can be compared to that of Jakov Lind's account which contributed to my own comments. Things I knew or have been told, for example, his reason for smoking Gauloises (see Section 3), are confirmed by Kiš. Friends appear under recognisable name changes, and and two indeed under their own names: Luba Jurgenson and Anka Dastre Rawicz, who appears as Noémie Dastre, a combination of her own maiden name and the first name of Boris's girl friend.

Novac, Ana, *Le Maître de trésor*, Editions du Rocher, 2002

'Mon livre sur Piotr', as she wrote in my copy.

Articles or chapters about the work of Piotr Rawicz

Alexander, Edward, *The Resonance of Dust: Essays on Holocaust Literature and Jewish Fate*, Ohio State University Press, 1979

Bougault, Laurence, 'Genres de l'histoire: l'exemple du *Sang du ciel* de Piotr Rawicz', in the proceedings of the colloquium *L'Histoire et la géographie dans le récit poétique*, CRLMC, Université Blaise Pascal, Clermont-Ferrand, 1997

Dayan Rosenman, Anny, 'Piotr Rawicz, la Douleur d'écrire', *Les Temps modernes*, March–April, 1995

Jaron, Steven, 'At the Edge of Humanity: The Dismissal of Historical Truth in Piotr Rawicz's Novel *Le Sang du ciel*', in *The Conscience of Humankind: Literature and Traumatic Experiences*, Elrud Ibsch and others (eds), Rodopi, Amsterdam, 2000

Katz Hewetson, Janina, 'Piotr Rawicz, pisarz zapomniany', *Kultura*, 3, Paris, 1990

Kauffmann, Judith, 'Langage de la violence et violence du langage: *La Shoa* dans *Le Sang du ciel* de Piotr Rawicz', *Hebrew University Studies in Literature and the Arts*, 20, 1993

Leclair Bertrand, 'Pour Piotr Rawicz, à l'heure des Bienveillantes', Oct 2006, www.remue.net

Solotaroff, Theodore, 'Anna Langfus and Piotr Rawicz' in *The Red Hot Vacuum*, Godine, 19

'The most freely created and brilliant treatment of the ontological issues that I know of in this literature. It seems less like a novel than a testament that has been written under aspell – so esoteric and multiple and yet so coherent is Rawicz's imagination of the Jewish terror and the world's disaster'.

Von Schwerin, Christoph Graf, 'Piotr Rawicz', *Twórczosc*, Warsaw, 44/6, 1998

Books containing brief references to Piotr Rawicz

Alvarez, A., 'The Literature of the Holocaust' in *Beyond All This Fiddle*, Random House, 1968

DeKoven Ezrahi, Sidra, *By Words Alone: the Holocaust in Literature*, University of Chicago Press, 1980

Friedlander, Albert H, *Riders Towards the Dawn*, Constable, 1992

Howe, Irving, 'Writing and the Holocaust' in *Writing and the Holocaust*, (edited by B. Lang), Holmes and Maier, 1988

Jaron, Steven, 'Judaism' in *Columbia History of Twentieth Century French Thought* (edited by Lawrence Kritzman), Columbia University Press, 2006

Lind, Jakov, *Crossing*, Methuen, 1991

Rose, Jacqueline, *The Haunting of Sylvia Plath*, Virago Press, 1991

Rosenfeld, Alvin, *A Double Dying: Reflections on Holocaust Literature*, Indiana University Press, 1980

Rudolf, Anthony, *At an Uncertain Hour: Primo Levi's War against Oblivion*, Menard Press, 1990

Rudolf, Anthony, *Wine from Two Glasses: Trust and Mistrust in Language*, Adam Archive Publications, 1991

Rudolf, Anthony, *I'm not even a Grownup: The Diary of Jerzy Feliks Urman*, Menard/Kings College, 1991

Stiffel, Frank, *The Tale of the Ring: A Kaddish*, Bantam Books, 1985

Taylor, John, *Paths to Contemporary French Literature*, Transaction Publishers, 2006

Teichman, Milton and Leder, Sharon, *Truth and Lamentations: Stories and Poems of the Holocaust*, University of Illinois Press, 1994

Wiesel, Elie, *Memoirs* (Vol. 1): *All Rivers Run to the Sea*, Knopf, 1995
'I see Piotr in front of me: tall, his wiry frame slightly stooped, his gaze a mixture of irony and desperation. I will speak of him, and of his death, later.'

Wiesel, Elie, *Memoirs* (Vol. 2): *And the Sea is Never Full*, Knopf, 1999
Contains a short section on the suicides of Primo Levi, Jerzy Kosinski and Piotr Rawicz.

Young, James, *Writing and Rewriting the Holocaust: Narrative and the Consequences of Interpretation*, Indiana University Press, 1990

Obituaries of Piotr Rawicz

Czapski, Jozef, *Kultura*, no 7/418–8/419, July–August, 1982

Kupferman, Jeanette, *European Judaism*, no 30, 1982

Piatier, Jacqueline, *Le Monde*, 25 May, 1982

Reviews of Piotr Rawicz's books

Le Sang du ciel

Bloch-Michel, Jean, *La Gazette de Lausanne*, 9 October 1961

Nadeau, Maurice, *L'Express*, 26 October 1961

Piatier, Jacqueline, *Le Monde*, 21 October 1961

Bloc-notes d'un contre-révolutionnaire

Baudy, Nicolas, *Nouveaux Cahiers*, Summer 1969

Blot, Jean, *La Gazette de Lausanne*, 6 September 1969

Cixous, Hélène, *Le Monde*, 31 May 1969

Milosz, Czeslaw, *Kultura*, 10/265, 1969

Other texts concerning Piotr Rawicz

Mitgang, Herbert, 'Portrait of Helen Wolff', *The New Yorker*, 2 August, 1982

The legendary publisher explains why she took on *Le Sang du ciel* and other book.

Rosenshield, Gary, 'Socialist Realism and the Holocaust: Jewish Life and Death in Anatoly Rybakov's *Heavy Sand*', *PMLA*, III/ 2, March 1996

Alludes to PR.

Rudolf, Anthony, letter, *Squiggle (Journal of Winnicott Studies)*, No 8, 1994

Reply to Adam Phillips. Brief discussion, mentioning PR, of concept of evil in Judaism.

Private letters: including Helen Wolff to AR, 24 September 1982; PR to Claude Vigée (see Section 3 for a translation of the letter), 13 January 1968; PR to Ernst Sello (undated); PR to AR (various); and letters to AR from several persons named in the acknowledgments, including A. Schwarz-Bart: see Section 3 for translation of part of the letter.

Books and articles about the backgound of Piotr Rawicz

Améry, Jean, *At the Mind's Limits: Contemplations by a Survivor on Auschwitz and its Realities*, Schocken, 1986

Antelme, Robert, *L'Espèce humaine*, Gallimard, 1978

Antelme, Robert, *The Human Race*, Marlboro Press, Vermont, 1992

See also, *Lignes* no 21, January 1994

Special issue devoted to Robert Antelme.

Appelfeld, Aharon, *The Age of Wonders*, Godine, 1981 (and other books)

Aronson, Ronald, *The Dialectics of Disaster: a Preface to Hope*, Verso Editions, 1983

Aronson, Ronald, *After Marxism*, The Guilford Press, 1995

Barthes, Roland, *The Rustle of Language*, Blackwells, 1986

Begley, Louis, *Wartime Lies*, Picador, 1992

Bernstein, Michael Andre, *Foregone Conclusions: Against Apocalyptic History*, University of California Press, 1994

Blanchot, Maurice, *The Writing of the Disaster*, University of Nebraska Press, 1986

Borowski, Tadeusz, *This Way to the Gas, Ladies and Gentlemen*, Penguin, 1980

Brown, Norman O., *Apocalypse and/or Metamorphosis*, University of California Press, 1991

Camus, Albert, *La Chute*, Gallimard, 1956

Canary, R. H. and Kozicki, H. (eds), *The Writing of History, Literary Form and Historical Understanding*, University of Wisconsin Press, 1978

Celan, Paul, *Poems*, translation by Michael Hamberger, Anvil Press, 1988 and 1995

The poem from which the Celan extract in 'Six Thoughts for Piotr Rawicz' is taken is not translated by Michael Hamburger. It is quoted in Jacques Derrida's essay on Celan – see below. After discussion with Michael Hamburger I have revised Derrida's translator's version.

Celan, Paul, *Selected Poems and Prose*, translation by John Felstiner, Norton, 2001

See also, Felstiner, John, *Paul Celan: Poet, Survivor, Jew*, Yale University Press, 1995

Cioran, E. M.

See Frank, Joseph, 'Thinkers and Liars', review article of *An Infamous Past: E. M. Cioran and the Rise of Fascism in Romania* by Marta Petreu, Ivan R. Dee, 2006 and of *Cioran, Eliade, Ionesco: L'oubli du fascisme* by Alexandra Laignel-Lavastine, 2002

Cohen, Arthur A., *The Tremendum: a Theological Interpretation of the Holocaust*, Crossroad, 1981

Cohen, Asher, Gelber, Joav and Wardi, Charlotte (eds), *Comprehending the Holocaust*, Verlag Peter Lang, Frankfurt am Main, 1988

Davis, Philip, *The Experience of Reading*, Routledge and Kegan Paul, 1992

Deguy, Michel (ed.), *Au Sujet de Shoah*, Bélin, 1990

Deguy, Michel, *Aux Heures d'affluences*, Le Seuil, 1993

Deleuze, Gilles, *Spinoza: Practical Philosophy*, City Lights Books, 1988

Derrida, Jacques, 'Shibboleth for Paul Celan' in *Word Traces: Readings of Paul Celan*, ed. Fioretos, Aris, Johns Hopkins University Press, 1994

Des Forêts, Louis René, *Le Bavard*, Gallimard, 1946

Des Forêts, Louis René, *The Children's Room*, John Calder, 1963

Contains a translation of *Le Bavard*.

Drix, Samuel, *Witness to Annihilation*, Brassey's, 1994

Duras, Marguerite, *La Douleur*, Fontana, 1986

See also follow-up obituary note about Robert Antelme by AR, *The Independent*, 14 March 1996

Encyclopaedia Judaica, Keter, Jerusalem, 1970
Can be consulted for more details on several topics, including a few cited in my text.

Encyclopaedia of the Jewish Diaspora (L'wow volume, 'The Destruction of the Jews of L'wow', ed. Philip Friedman), Jerusalem, 1956

Fishman, Charles (ed.), *Blood to Remember: American Poets on the Holocaust*, Texas Tech University Press, 1991

See also review of above book by Anthony Rudolf, *American Book Review*, Vol. 15, no 1, New York, April/May, 1993

Friedlander, Albert H., 'Misuses of the Holocaust', *European Judaism*, no 32, 1983

Friedrich, Otto, *The Kingdom of Auschwitz*, Penguin, 1996

Gascar, Pierre, *Les Bêtes et le temps des morts*, Gallimard, 1953

Gilbert, Martin, *The Holocaust (the Jewish Tragedy)*, Fontana, 1987
Contains several sections of the testimony of Rudolf Reder, one of the two survivors of Belzec.

Gombrowicz, Witold, *Pornografia*, Penguin, 1991

Heimler, Eugene, *Night of the Mist*, Vanguard Press, New York, 1959 (and other books)

Hertz, J. H. (ed.), *The Pentateuch and Haftorahs*, Soncino Press, 1956

Herzog, Henry Armin, *. . . And Heaven Shed No Tears*, Menard Press, 1996

Hill, Geoffrey, *Collected Poems*, Penguin, 1985

Himmelfarb, Gertrude, 'Telling it as you like it: post-modern History and the flight from fact', *TLS*, 19 October, 1992

Jewish Publication Society of America, *The Holy Scriptures according to the Masoretic Text*, 1985

Kafka, Franz, 'In the Penal Settlement', in *Metamorphosis and other Stories*, Penguin, 1961

Kaplan, Chaim A., *Warsaw Diary*, Collier Books, 1973

Katzetnik 135633, *House of Dolls*, Simon & Schuster, 1955 (and other books)

Kiš, Danilo, *Hourglass*, Faber and Faber, 1990

Kiš, Danilo, *Homo Poeticus: Essays and Interviews*, Carcanet, 1996

Kitaj, R. B., *Catalogue of Little Pictures*, Marlborough Gallery, London, 2006

See also Catalogue of Retrospective Exhibition ed. R. Morphet, Tate Gallery, 1994

See also Livingstone, M., *R. Kitaj*, Phaidon, 1985

See also Kinsman, J., *Kitaj Prints*, Scolar Press, 1994

See also Rios, Julian, *Kitaj: Pictures and Conversations*, Hamish Hamilton, 1994

Kosinski, Jerzy, *The Painted Bird*, Houghton Mifflin, 1976
This, the second edition, contains an important introduction by the author.

Kosinski, Jerzy, *The Hermit of 69th Street*, Zebra Books, 1991

See also 'Kosinski's War' by James Park Sloan, *The New Yorker*, October 10, 1994

See also review by C. Lehmann-Haupt of James Park Sloan's biography of Kosinski, *New York Times*, 28 February, 1996

See also review by Louis Begley of James Park Sloan's biography of Kosinski, *New York Times*, Sunday April 21, 1996

Lanzmann, Claude, *Shoah*, Fayard, 1985

Lanzmann, Claude (interview by AR), *London Magazine*, June/July, 1994

Levene, Mark, 'Is the Holocaust simply another example of Genocide?', *Patterns of Prejudice*, Vol. 28/2, Institute of Jewish Affairs, 1994

Levi, Primo, *The Drowned and the Saved*, Michael Joseph, 1988 (and other books)

Lind, Jakov, *Soul of Wood*, Jonathan Cape, 1964 (and other books)

Lustig, Arnost, *Lovely Green Eyes*, Arcade, 2002 (and other books)

Maccoby, Hyam, *The Sacred Executioner*, Thames and Hudson, 1982

In my text, I refer to Chapter 7, 'Moses and Circumcision'; the retranslated passage is on page 89. See also the article on circumcision in the *Encyclopaedia Judaica*.

Maybaum, Ignaz, *Jewish Existence*, Vallentine Mitchell, 1960

Maybaum, Ignaz, *Creation and Guilt*, Vallentine Mitchell, 1969

Milosz, Czeslaw, *The Witness of Poetry*, Harvard University Press, 1983

Morse, Jonathan, *Word by Word: the Language of Memory*, Cornell University Press, 1990

Morse, Jonathan, 'Words devoted to the Unspeakable', *American Literary History*, Winter, 1993

Music, Zoran, *L'Oeuvre graphique*, Centre G. Pompidou, 1988

Music, Zoran, *Dessins*, Weber, 1973

See also 'Seeing into the Life of Things', Steven Jaron's Adam Lecture for 2006 (forthcoming)

Nadeau, Maurice, *The History of Surrealism*, Jonathan Cape, 1968

Oppen, George, *New Collected Poems*, New Directions, 2002

Oppenheimer, Paul, 'Mass Death and Resurrection', *The Jewish Quarterly*, Vol. 43/1, Spring, 1996

Peleg-Marianska, Miriam and Peleg, Mordecai, *Witnesses: Life in Occupied Cracow*, Routledge and Kegan Paul, 1991

Perkal, Max, *Outside was Beautiful: The Notebooks of a 19-year-old Jew written in 1945*, Menard Press, 1996

This memoir also contains the original text, written in a mixture of German and Yiddish.

Polizzotti, Mark, *Revolution of the Mind: the Life of Andre Breton*, Bloomsbury, 1995

Potok, Chaim, *The Gift of Asher Lev*, Fawcett Crest, 1990

Presser, Jacques, *The Night of the Girondists*, Harvill, 1992

Contains an introduction by Primo Levi.

Read, Herbert (ed.), *Surrealism*, Faber and Faber, 1936

Ringelblum, E., *Notes from the Warsaw Ghetto*, McGraw Hill, 1958

Rosenfeld, Alvin, 'Popularisation and Memory: The Case of Anne Frank', in *Lessons and Legacies: The Meaning of the Holocaust in a Changing World*, edited by Peter Hayes, Northwestern University Press, Evanston, 1991

Roskies, David, *Against the Apocalypse: Responses to Catastrophe in Modern Jewish Culture*, Harvard University Press, 1984

Rubenstein, Richard L., *After Auschwitz: Radical Theology and Contemporary Judaism*, Bobbs-Merrill, 1966

Rudolf, Anthony, 'Pikolo, Primo Levi's 'The Mensch' and three great poems', *Poetry Nation Review*, No 92, Manchester, 1993 (shorter version published in *The Independent*, 26 March, 1993)

Rudolf, Anthony, 'Rescue Work: Memory and Text', *Stand*, Leeds, 5 (3), 2004

Samuel, Jean, *L'Homme face à l'univers concentrationnaire*, Rotary Colmar, 1985

Scarpetta, Guy, *L'age d'or du roman*, Grasset, 1996
Chapter on *Sablier* by D. Kiš , with no mention of Rawicz's preface. Scarpetta is also editor in chief of *La Règle du jeu* which published Kiš 's story about Rawicz. See Note A in Section 2.

Schenk McCord, Janet, 'The psychache of Primo Levi and Jerzy Kosinski', *The Journal of Psychology and Judaism*, New York, January/February 1994
Special issue on suicide and Judaism.

Schulz, Bruno, *Sanatorium under the Sign of the Crocodile*, Picador, 1980

Schulz, Bruno, *Street of Crocodiles*, Picador, 1980

Schwarz-Bart, André, *The Last of the Just*, Penguin, 1977

Searle, John, letter in *New York Review of Books*, XLII, 20, 21 Dec. 1995

Sinclair, Clive, *Bedbugs*, Allison and Busby, 1982 (and other books)

Sommer Lefkovits, Elisabeth, *Are you here in this Hell too?: Memories of Troubled Times* 1944–1945, Menard Press, 1996

Sutton, Nina, *Bruno Bettelheim, The Other Side of Madness*, Duckworth, 1995

Szende, S., *The Promise Hitler Kept*, Gollancz, 1945

Szwajger, Adina, *I Remember Nothing More: The Warsaw Children's Hospital and the Jewish Resistance*, Harvill, 1993

Thalmann, Rita and Feinermann, Emmanuel, *Crystal Night*, Thames and Hudson, 1974

Thorne, Leon, *Out of the Ashes*, Bloch, 1976

Tomkiewicz, Mina, *There was Life even There*, Polskaya Fundacja Kulturna, 1991

Vidal-Naquet, Pierre, *Les Assassins de la mémoire*, La Découverte, 1987

Vigée, Claude, translation by Anthony Rudolf, *Flow Tide: Selected Poetry and Prose*, Menard/Kings College London, 1992

Wells, Leon W., *The Janowska Road* (*The Death Brigade*), Holocaust Library, 1978

Wells, Leon W., 'I do not say Kaddish', in *Conservative Judaism*, Vol XXXI, 4, Summer 1977

White H., *The Context of Form: Narrative Discourse and Historical Representation*, Johns Hopkins University Press, Baltimore, 1989 (and other books)

Wiesel, Elie, *Night*, Hill and Wang, 1960 (and other books)

(Wilson, Angus), *Angus Wilson: a Bibliography* 1947–1987 by J. H. Stape and A. N. Thomas, Mansell, 1988

Yerushalmi, Yosef Hayim, *Zakhor: Jewish History and Jewish Memory*, University of Washington Press, 1983

Appendix

Yale University Press reprinted the original 1964 translation unrevised in 2003. This omits ten brief passages from Rawicz's French text as published by Gallimard in 1961. These have been incorporated in my revised translation published by Elliott and Thompson in 2004. For more information, see the bibliography, the new Introduction and Note 14 to Section 2 of the present work. Here are two particularly interesting passages that may be of interest to readers of the Yale edition or indeed those who possess or borrow the 1964 translation.

1

In Chapter 1, on page 4 of the 1964 translation and page 4 of the Yale Edition, the following extract from pages 10–11 of the original French was omitted. It should be inserted immediately after the words: '. . . is beginning to take place on the horizon'. I offer three versions of the poem, each attempting in different ways to convey the sense and the rhyme. The original French goes:

Horizon?
Quel affront!

Concerning horizon, a little poem springs to mind. Don't worry. This little poem is very short, only two lines. It was dedicated to an Academician, a member of the Academy, a member . . . well . . .

Hint of a setting: he wakes up, this member, he rises, he looks all around him and speaks the poem:

Horizon's light?
What a slight!

or

Sky-line?
Insult to your bye-line!

or (the best)

Light on the horizon?
Shame to set your eyes on!

You don't like my poem? Too bad. Let's go on:

Continue on page four with 'My shop is open . . .'

2

In Chapter 16, on page 135 of the 1964 translation and page 135 of the Yale edition, the following extract from page 121 of the original French was omitted. It should be inserted immediately after the words 'In escaping from the town?' The motto is an awkward couplet, in Russian in the original French edition of the book. I have slightly re-transliterated it for the English ear. Russian experts could not identify it. One hazarded it might be from an anonymous prison song. Or Rawicz could have invented it.

Motto:
Ya vsyo, ya vsyo vam rasskazhou
V tyomnom rodilsya ya ouglou . . .
[I'll tell you all, I'll tell you all
In a dark place was I born . . .]

The Upanishad, crazy, alive . . .
(But is one obliged to give the name 'life' to that complicated gasping imposed by the Creator?)

Continue on page 135 with 'Condemned as I am to . . . '

Acknowledgements

Various intimates, friends and acquaintances of Piotr Rawicz and his wife, around the world, spoke to me on and off the record. They ranged from those who answered all my questions and more, to those who preferred to say nothing (who are not named) but all, including those who said nothing, without exception honoured the project and were pleased that, after a long period of neglect, attention once again is being focussed on a literary masterpiece and its complex creator. In Section 3 I have tried to convey something of the presence of the man in his world, but I must insist that his friends did not always see eye to eye about this and that, and none of them would necessarily agree with the provisionally final shape of my thought processing. I thank: Juliette Bazin, Rabbi Lionel Blue, Aurora Cornea, John Faulds, Michele Forgeois, Evelyn and the late Rabbi Albert Friedlander, Mira Hammamersh, Cecil Helman, Ze'ev Ben-Shlomo, Luba Jurgenson, the late Hugnet Karvellis, Jeanetta Kupferman, the late Wanda Ladniewska, the late Helena Lecalot, Jakov Lind, Hans Maier, Ana Novac, Maggie Pioro, the late Julian and Miriam Reiss, Zofia Romanowicz, Claude Royet-Journoud, Mr and Mrs Rudnicki, Brenda Rudolf, the late Andre Schwarz-Bart, Gabriela and the late Christoph Graf Schwerin von Schwanenfeld, Hélène Senn, Frank Stiffel, the late Lucy Ulrych, Eric Vaux, Claude Vigée and Leon Weliczer Wells.

I also want to thank Zbigniew Kotowicz and the late Felek Scharf for reading Polish texts with me; Zwi Rosenwasser for reading a Hebrew text with me; Michael Hamburger for a discussion about one particular Celan poem (see Note in Bibliography under Celan); Fay Bussgang, Marcel Cohen, Jean-Pierre Dauphin, John Felstiner, Jacky Goulston, Michael Heller, Mark Hutchinson, Steve Light, Anna Marianska, Miriam and Motti Neiger, Françoise Ragot, Vicki Rosenberg, Anne Serre, Nina Sutton, Elie Wiesel and Dan Weissbort for sending texts or information difficult to find in London; Aharon Appelfeld, Paul Auster, Lucia Levi, Margaret Drabble, Martin Gilbert, the late

Hyam Maccoby, Natasha Franklin, Elizabeth James, Barry Davis, Jonathan Webber and Zinovi Zinik for confirming or clarifying a few details; Sergei Kravtsov for his exceptional kindness in digging around the L'wow archives just before his final departure for Jerusalem and coming up with part of Piotr's student file, and to his friend Ilya Levin for the photo of the apartment block; the late Czeslaw Milosz for information and for sending me his poem, co-translated with Robert Hass, on Piotr's late wife, Anka Dastre Rawicz; Claude Lanzmann and Jean and Claude Samuel for their generous help while I was in France; the late Max Sebald for the invitation, suggested by Clive Sinclair, to speak at his seminar on Holocaust literature at the University of East Anglia, which led to the second draft of Section 1 of this book – and to all present on that occasion for their constructive comments; Dan Franklin then of Secker and Warburg, the late Giles Gordon then of Sheil Lang and, long before that, of Secker and Warburg, Peter Wiles and Messrs Gallimard for advice concerning original publication both of the text and of the translation and to whom I make copyright acknowledgments – as well as to Rawicz's literary executor, his nephew Andre Garcianda; *European Judaism* which published three of my translations of Rawicz prose; *Tel-Aviv Review*, which published my poem to Gisèle Celan-Lestrange; Janet Berg in Jerusalem for organising the Hebrew setting for the frontispiece; finally, the friends who commented on early drafts of parts of the essays: David Elliott, Musa Moris Farhi, Eva Hoffmann, James Hogan, Merlin James, Alan Wall and, especially, Barbara Garvin.

I would like to say that John Felstiner's long engagement with the work of Celan and Michael Heller's with that of the Objectivist poets continue to serve as a model and inspiration. The art of R. B. Kitaj has always accompanied my thoughts in this territory. I would like to thank him for his generosity in offering the use of any of his work in any form as a frontispiece – I originally chose his portrait entitled 'The Marrano' because this is what Boris, the hero or anti-hero of Rawicz's book, has to succeed in being in order to survive, and also because unknown to Kitaj, who has or had not yet read *Blood from the Sky*, there is something of Boris in the characterisation of the portrait. But in the end I decided upon his marvellous lithograph of Abraham from *Bible Portraits* (1992). My reasons are made clear in the book. For the second edition, a timely exhibition at the Marlborough Gallery gave me a perfect image to use on the new cover: 'Expulsion', (2006). Thanks are due to Sarah Staughton formerly of the Marlborough's Graphics department, to Frankie Rossi and Geoffrey Parton.

I end this necessarily long list of acknowledgments with a special one to the original translator of the novel, Peter Wiles, and I quote from his letter to me of 26 March 1993, because it is not every book which yields such a strong and beautiful reaction; may his words encourage all readers of the present work to give serious attention to my arguments, and then turn to the novel itself as soon as possible: 'It was the most difficult book I ever translated and some of its horrors cost me a bit in brandy, but it was full of wonders and continues to haunt me after thirty years'.